# SOCIETY, DICHOTOMIES AND RESOLUTIONS

For my Grandparents Grace, Gren, Marjorie and also Fred who would have been disappointed that the book is not about Hegel.

# Society, Dichotomies and Resolutions

An inquiry into social synthesis

LUCY FRITH
*St Martin's College*
*Lancaster*

# Avebury

Aldershot · Brookfield USA · Hong Kong · Singapore · Sydney

Published by
Avebury
Ashgate Publishing Limited
Gower House
Croft Road
Aldershot
Hants GU11 3HR
England

Ashgate Publishing Company
Old Post Road
Brookfield
Vermont 05036
USA

**British Library Cataloguing in Publication Data**

Frith, Lucy
    Society, Dichotomies and Resolutions: Inquiry into
    Social Synthesis — (Avebury Series in Philosophy)
    I. Title    II. Series
    301.01

ISBN 1 85628 281 3

Printed and Bound in Great Britain by
Athenaeum Press Ltd, Newcastle upon Tyne.

# Contents

# Acknowledgements

I would like to thank all those who read the manuscript Melanie Baigel, Anita Sumner, Elliot Perry and Trevor Curnow for their comments and suggestions. I would particularly like to thank David Lamb whose support, humour and critical comments has helped me immeasurably.

I am indebted to my father, who proof read the manuscript many times and was very patient with me when I did not deserve it. I would also like to thank Annabel Lermer for her constant encouragement and my mother and sister for being generally supportive. Finally, those who have helped with the preparation and typing deserve a special mention, particularly Julie Robinson for her patience.

# Introduction

Individualism is an oft and widely used concept, which has received particular exposure in the 1980s, advanced as the theoretical basis of New Right conservatism, popularly known as Thatcherism. It is frequently argued that former prime minister Margaret Thatcher forged a new direction in British politics, overturning the previous collectivist consensus and replacing it with free-market economics and rigorous individualism. Due to such policy measures Thatcherism has now achieved the status of a coherent political ideology, representing a dramatic reversal of post-war politics. This is an interpretation of the Thatcher years that is shared by many political commentators. David Marquand sums up this view of Thatcherism:

> The fortresses of the post-war settlement - trade unions, universities, nationalised industries, local authorities - were systematically humbled....In place of paternalist collectivism, the Thatcherites offered authoritarian individualism: free choice in the market place and hierarchy everywhere else. (Marquand,1990:21)

Under Thatcher's administration collectivist measures were called into question, public services and state provision for those unable to help themselves were dramatically reduced, and the very idea that these were the responsibility of the state was questionned. An extreme version of "Thatcherite" philosophy, as elucidated by David Marquand, was advocated by the "No Turning Back" group of the Conservative Party, who went so far as to advance the complete abolition of the welfare state. In order to facilitate this shifting pattern of welfare responsibility, there was an attempt to change the value structure of society in tandem with the economic framework. The "Thatcherites" reintroduced individualism into the political vocabulary, creating from its basic premises a different doctrine, often heralded as the New Right, a

1

blend of free-market economics, Manchester liberalism and traditional conservative authoritarianism.

With the advent of John Major's premiership, there has been much debate over the existence of ideological differences and similarities between Thatcher and her successor. An initial difference, often cited, is that there was no coherent ideological package that could be characterized as Majorism in the same way that there was a doctrine of Thatcherism, (as indeed Mrs Thatcher stated herself). As a newspaper article stated: "Shortly after he became Prime Minister [John Major] let it be known that Central Office was not to use the term Majorism in briefings. He was a pragmatic figure, ill suited to "isms", intent on taking each issue on its rational ideological merits." (Wintour,1991) However, in his speech to the Conservative Party conference in Blackpool, Autumn 1991, Major continually highlighted the importance of the individual, both as the conceptual root of Conservative ideology and as a means of social organization. "Old though our party is, the values behind it are older still. They are rooted in the instincts of every individual, and it is through our policies that we make them come alive." And, "I want to give individuals greater control over their own lives....Every family, the right to have and to hold their own private corner of life; their own home, their own savings, their own security for their future - and for their children's future." (Major,1991) These points illustrate that Major has not abandoned the Thatcherite concern for the individual and hence retained one of the central ideological planks of the Thatcher Government. Such events in contemporary politics renew the relevancy of discussions on individualism and the practical implications of the doctrine.

Individualism, is itself, a well-established doctrine, encouraged rather than created by the Conservative Government which took office in 1979. The concept of individualism examined here has a long history originating in the nineteenth century and has evolved gradually (as have concepts such as socialism and communism) into the doctrine as we understand it today. Hence, over time its exact meaning has changed considerably, from its use as an epithet for nonconformity in religion to the methodological connotations it has now. Individualism as a methodological concept developed hand in hand with liberalism, its political counterpart, each linked in a supporting reciprocal relationship.

This work inquires into the nature of individualism but does not, and cannot, fully address the many different doctrines into which it can be subdivided.[1] The term "individualism" is used throughout to encompass doctrines that emerge as a result of conceiving individuals as abstract entities. The methodological and epistemological facets follow directly from this notion of an abstract individual. It must be stressed that this is not a study of one subdivision of the concept but an examination of individualism in its broadest sense.

The formulation of the concept of individualism is illuminated by putting it in a wider and more diverse context than it is commonly placed in, that is, not locating it solely within the confines of political

2

philosophy. By examining how individualism influences all branches of knowledge, not solely social and political theory, the implicit assumptions behind the doctrine of individualism can be clarified. When placed in a broader context it is possible to see that individualism is based on implicit assumptions about human nature. Traditionally, individualism has been regarded as an expression of people's natural essence and this was unquestionably accepted in many discussions concerning the validity of the concept. The main concern of this book, however, is the theory of human nature that underpins individualism. This tacitly accepted theory should not be taken as an unproblematic given and needs to be subjected to analysis. This issue is considered and developed in Chapter One.

Individualism, along with liberalism, has managed to win credence by dressing itself in the mantle of undisputed fact. The philosophy of liberal democracy from Locke onwards has been based on the belief that it is the political outcome of natural human organizational tendencies. In this way liberalism is able to claim that it is a value-free and necessary form of social organization. It facilitates this by building on two assumptions. First, individualism arises because it is held to be the natural outcome of human nature. This form of human nature is portrayed as fundamentally static and similar in all contexts, although the environment may be acknowledged as providing a slight and marginal influence - albeit a passing one. Taking this basic nature, exponents of individualism have constructed a political theory around what they considered to be natural for humans, a theory which does not go against the grain of the inherent human essence. Second, by building on a positivist and empiricist theory of science, exponents of these theories are able to claim that individualism is a universal concept.

The former point will form the basis of the book. If it can be proved that this static and abstract conception of human nature underpins theories of individualism and, further, that this theory of human nature can be shown to be untenable or at least a theory specific to Western culture, then there are good grounds for claiming that individualism's status as a universal theory can and should be refuted. The notion of individualism as a representation of natural essence can be problematized by showing how it has been historically constructed within a certain culture. Once such an historical specificity has been established, this formulation of human nature can be subjected to critical analysis, a task that is long overdue as it has generally been tacitly, and therefore unproblematically, accepted as universally true.

This abstract and static theory of human nature has ramifications for the debate between the two rival schools of social explanation; individualism and collectivism. An adherence to this theory of human nature results in the stalemate that the debate over the scope of social explanation has reached. This stalemate is due to the conflicting theories of human nature that each doctrine is premised on resulting in an inability to agree on fundamental terms. Therefore, an elucidation of the individualistic theory of human nature can highlight the salient areas of contention

3

between the two doctrines. Further, the difficulties in adequately theorizing social influence (that is often such a problematic task in social theory) can be explained by reference to this abstract theory of human nature. This problem of theorizing social influence is examined in Chapter Two.

Accordingly, it is possible to locate individualism in a specific social and political context; as an ideological construct, rather than as an exposition of a true and concrete reality. The methodology of empiricist science and the abstract theory of human nature have to be examined from a critical viewpoint and not accepted unquestionably. Individualism has operated as a persuasive ideological construct and depends for its acceptance and validity on the grounds that it is a factual and true theory. The political ramifications of such a position are clear: from such an objectivist stance it can be claimed that rival doctrines to liberalism, such as socialism, conflict with what is deemed to be naturally possible for humanity. These collectivist doctrines are seen as aberrations from what humanity really *is* and such measures could go against the grain of people's inherent essence. In this way collectivist doctrines have often been cast in the role of alien forms of social organization imposed on human nature by social engineering theorists.[2] Yet, if human nature was static and conformed to the abstract individualist formulation it would indeed falsify collectivist doctrines. Thus, individualism expressed as a political doctrine has weakened the position of its opponents by portraying their measures as foreign and unnatural and has strengthened its own position by masquerading as objective fact. This carries with it the practical problem that political ends can be operated on behalf of certain interests, without these interests being made explicitly known. For example, liberalism as a political doctrine has tended to operate in the interests of the bourgeoisie, while claiming impartiality and universal applicability to all sectors of society.

A further element of individualism requiring explanation is the centrality of the subject in analysis, a methodological construct that forms the bedrock of liberalism and humanism. Within this centrality, the individual is the locus of causation and occupies the primary role in knowledge creation. This is a reductionist position whereby the individual is seen to be the only moving agent and therefore the only appropriate area for study; the individual becomes the "subject" of social explanation deposing any amalgamated constructs. If this positioning was reversed and collectivist structures relocated to a central place in analysis, it is argued that a number of problematic consequences would result. Humanists claim it would be detrimental to individual freedom; once the individual is deprived of this central role, then individual rights could easily become secondary to collective rights and the rights of society. Thus, it is frequently suggested by exponents of individualism that this subordination of the individual to the collective could lead to totalitarianism, and fears are expressed about the creation of a controlling and deterministic society, in which there is no basis or safeguard for individual rights.[3] Due to these fears, society or collectives

4

must be seen as the amalgam of individual wants, aims and behaviour, otherwise the individual could be neglected in favour of pursuing the interests of the collective.

It will be contended that just the reverse is the case: that to perceive society as comprising many separate, unrelated individuals could lead (as it was arguably shown under the Thatcher administration) to a decrease in freedoms, particularly as a result of state withdrawal from the economic sphere in favour of private monopolies. Much of the legislation passed during that Conservative term of office (1979-1991) was designed to remove state intervention, these policies being justified on the grounds that they would increase personal freedom. However, such legislation has in fact reduced those very freedoms which depend on collective security. For instance, the legal curbs on collective bargaining, extending to the withdrawal of labour, resulted in a decrease in workers' freedom, because they were restricted in the industrial action they could legally take; and the abolition of wages councils, allowing employers to impose lower rates of pay, had a detrimental effect on poorly organised workers.

To create a society where no one feels obliged to help others, when collective values associated with citizenship are replaced by individualist notions of consumerism, where scarce resources are not divided according to mutual needs but according to the ability to pay and the concept of a free health service is questioned, is hardly a step down the road to continued freedom. Exponents of liberalism and individualism have defined freedom in a negative fashion, namely, freedom consists of an absence of controls. Once it is defined in this way, any form of intervening legislation or action, even if it was designed to bring about equality (minimum wages for example) would be defined as an infringement of negative freedom. Negative freedom cannot guarantee civil liberties, (although it is an essential precursor), it is not enough simply to state that we are all equal individuals, and should be treated as such, unless there are structures to bring this about. It is meaningless, for example, to talk about education for all if there are no methods to enable disadvantaged children to benefit from the system in the way their middle-class counterparts do.

The main tenet of this work is that the definition of the subject as constructed by individualism can and does lead to a decrease in social justice. This is the converse of the position adhered to by most proponents of individualism and liberalism. They argue that the strength of liberalism as a political doctrine is the ability to guarantee individual freedom and create a more equal society, whereas, I would claim that often quite the reverse is the case. I shall turn now to a brief clarification of these issues, to express exactly in what sense it is argued that the individualistic construction of the subject creates detrimental consequences for personal freedom.

Theories of individualism from Hobbes onwards have traditionally been concerned with the issue of personal freedom and this concern was incorporated into the basic principles of nineteenth-century liberalism.

5

This concept of freedom was inextricably linked to free-market relations, an economic system that was thought to preserve freedom by dint of its unhampered competitiveness, and notions of ownership, consisting of both property in oneself and property in material possessions. C B Macpherson highlights these points when he examines possessive individualism: "The individual is essentially the proprietor of his own person and capacities, for which he owes nothing to society. Hobbes...reduces the human essence to freedom from others' wills and proprietorship in one's own capacities." The Levellers also incorporated these assumptions into their theorizing: "The human essence is freedom from the will of other, and freedom is the function of the proprietorship of one's person." (Macpherson,1983:264 & 265) Modern political theorists have taken these seventeenth-century concepts of political obligation to argue against state intervention on the grounds that it would infringe personal freedom. Hayek, for instance, contends that not only would such intervention be coercive, it would also be an inferior mechanism of co-ordinating individual efforts; economic liberalism, "regards competition as superior not only because it is in most circumstances the most efficient method known, but even more because it is the only method by which our activities can be adjusted to each other without coercive or arbitrary intervention of authority." (Hayek,1986:27)

It is undeniable that social justice in the last two centuries has been considerably advanced by liberal ideas of each individual counting as one and equal in the eyes of the state and the legislature. Steven Lukes makes the point:

> I have also suggested that this way of conceiving the individual was historically progressive. It was a crucial weapon in the breaking down of traditional privileges and hierarchies, in the dissolution of separate and incommensurable social orders and ranks, and in the establishing of universal human claims in the form of legal rights. The formal legal framework of modern democratic society is the guardian of the abstract individual. It provides for formal equality (before the law) and formal freedom (from illegal or arbitrary treatment). (Lukes,1985:152-153)

However, it is not to these issues that this book addresses itself. While bearing in mind the liberatory results liberalism (and hence individualism) have achieved, it is with the not so positive aspects of individualism that the book is concerned. These are less often expounded and therefore deserve further attention. It is the operation of the basic tenets of individualism as universal truths, instead of the culturally specific constructs they arguably are, that is criticized in this discussion. The most pertinent of these concepts is the theory of human nature upon which individualism is based and its elevation to the status of an *a priori* truth. The historical formulation of this theory of human nature is discussed in Chapter Three.

It is important to clarify exactly which facets of individualism are criticized in this work. It is to the application of this concept that the bulk of the analysis is directed, namely its operation as a tacitly held ideology and the influence it has had on conceptions of humanity. There is only a limited critique of methodological individualism, the doctrine in its most austere form (see Chapter One), as it is not a concept that reflects modern societal arrangements in practice. Therefore, the more covert operations of individualism are given greater coverage. For instance, individualist conceptions of the subject can prejudice the adequate formulation of societal influence (considered in Chapter Two) and this results in social policy frequently not fully appreciating the social and collective nature of certain problems. In a sense this book aims to extend liberal and individualistic assumptions further in order to facilitate greater freedoms. Individualism has dealt with freedom on one level, the "freedom from"; a socially located analysis could address the "freedom to".

Freedom, even defined in a negative sense (the "freedom from") has made an important contribution and led to a much fairer society. However, by simply concentrating on this area, other equally important limitations of freedom are ignored, for instance, the pressures exerted by societal constructs and structures that restrict the freedom to do certain things are seldom considered, and these constraints cannot be redressed by solely concentrating on an individual level of analysis. It is individualism's construction of the subject that can lead to a denial of societal influences and hence a denial of certain constraints on freedom. This is illustrated by social psychology's treatment of racial prejudice in Chapter Three.

It is further argued that the inability to construct societal influence is not necessarily a problem that solely originates in only considering the individual, but it is also created by the formulation of the individual in an abstract unitary form. To concentrate on individuals and their wants and aims is not in itself unwarranted; it is seeing this individual as completely distinct from society that creates the problems and limitations highlighted. Chapter Four outlines ways of reformulating the subject so it can be more amenable to societal influence and enter into a more dynamic relationship with society as opposed to being classed as a distinct entity.

Another aspect of individualism that requires explanation is the mechanism by which the doctrine incorporates the assumptions of an empiricist theory of scientific investigation into its analysis, tacitly accepting this methodology without ever explicitly providing a justification. Unfortunately, space does not allow for a full consideration of individualism's underlying philosophy of science, hence the issue can only be treated briefly. Individualism builds on an empiricist theory of knowledge in so far as some versions assert that there is a concrete reality about which various truths can be ascertained and theories can be verified on scientific and objective grounds. This notion of scientific objectivity is an imposed one and must be challenged in order to mount an effective critique of individualism. Once theories are put in their historical context they can be viewed as socially constructed and individualism's appeal to universality rejected. Theorists began to give social factors a place in the determination of causation by moving away from objective justification, a justificatory methodology which developed in the seventeenth century with the emergence of a scientific and mechanistic world view. The move away from ideas formulated in the Enlightenment, ideas that attempted to elucidate general universal principles that could reveal a certain natural and social reality, have characterized much recent social theory drawing on the beginnings Marx founded to mount a more sustained attack. These theorizations have laid the foundations for twentieth-century social critique. This makes it possible to create a space for a wider analysis in the form of social constructionism, a position that has permeated all subjects, resulting in a greater depth of understanding. Building on this postmodernism goes beyond previous claims about the specificity of doctrines to their culture and challenges the very criteria by which knowledge is both legitimized and justified.

These moves away from scientific objectivity in social theory can be located in a broader context and the whole movement has often been characterized as a paradigm shift.[4] This new paradigm challenges more deeply the view of a reality that is unchanging and ultimately knowable. P Major-Poetzl, in a work considering Foucault's archaeology of knowledge, locates his theorizing within the context of such a paradigm shift:

> Innovations in the human sciences and fine arts not only indicate that the traditional paradigm is askew, as Kuhn puts it, but that parallel developments are occurring in many disciplines and that a new paradigm is emerging. While the Saussurian "revolution" in linguistics is perhaps the best example, innovations in psychology and anthropology reflect a similar shift away from developmental processes toward systematic relations. (Major-Poetzl, 1983:91)

Under this account, instead of formulating the social as the nexus of change and locating this in the prevailing scientific structures, the very structures themselves are challenged. The paradigm shift can be talked of in a Kuhnian way: once a current theory fails to provide an adequate description of reality, that is, when it cannot account for certain anomalies, the work of problem solving within the current paradigm (normal science) will cease and rival paradigms will begin to suggest themselves - then a new period can be entered into.

This has happened in physics where paradigm has replaced paradigm. The paradigm of classical mechanics, which held despite many reformulations until the beginning of the century, was undermined by the theory of relativity and has been gradually superseded by quantum mechanics. This can be used to provide an analogy for social theory. When the dominant paradigm that governed physics was rooted in objectivity and certainty, social theory attempted to ground itself in similar values. Now social theory is changing in response to the developments in physics. Consequently branches of knowledge cannot be totally separated as they arise out of the same social context.

Therefore, social theory is undergoing a paradigm change which, it can be argued, is very similar to developments in modern physics. Major-Poetzl articulates the link between all forms of knowledge and sees the new developments in all fields as forming part of this paradigm shift:

> Foucault's literary essays, structural linguistics, relativity theory, quantum mechanics, various "field" theories in the human sciences all point to "isomorphisms" in diverse disciplines which suggest the formation of a new paradigm. This paradigm replaces Newtonian-Cartesian conceptions of causality, time, space, subject, and object with systematic relations in which the subject is merely a variable function, objects have no fixed substance, space and time interact, and change is discontinuous. (Major-Poetzl, 1983:104)

This new paradigm gives social theory the means to move beyond simply positing societal influences within a conventional scientific discourse. The centrality given to the subject has to be removed and this cannot be done if positivist scientific frameworks are retained as the boundaries of reason. Theorists attempting this displacement of the subject such as Foucault, who employs an analysis founded on discourse and genealogy to adequately theorize the social, provide a useful way forward (see Chapter Four). Social theory needs reworking along the lines established in physics. Although a full examination of this paradigm shift is outside the boundaries of this book, it is sufficient to stress that there are alternatives being developed which challenge the hegemony of individualism, scientific objectivity and mechanism. Hence, the transience of doctrines such as individualism is finally being recognized.

In order to establish and illustrate these points a methodology will be employed which moves from the abstract to the practical illustrating how the abstract can have immense and discernible practical ramifications. The end result will hope to show that all these abstract philosophical constructs permeate down to the everyday life and organizational configurations of individuals. Due to the important political effects such theorization can have the use that is made of these theories should occupy an important place in the discussion. That is, when evaluating the acceptability of a theory, the societal arrangements that it could necessitate should be part of the criteria as well as epistemological and methodological considerations. In order to do this it is important to recognize that such theories are not necessarily true or objective nor indeed do such criteria have to be employed to pronounce some form of evaluation. Hence, the results of scientific projects could be taken into account when considering whether the research itself is a viable enterprise. Unwelcome effects of these projects could no longer be justified on the grounds that the scientist had no choice as s/he was simply pursuing knowledge to its logical conclusion. To use a crude example, developments such as the atomic bomb could have been avoided once the terrible consequences were known and its formulation not seen as the progression of knowledge along a set and unchangeable path.

Within this move from the abstract to the practical two areas will be considered, social philosophy and psychology; the introduction of the latter needs some clarification. Psychology will be considered because it attempts to both classify and characterize the individual and specifically examines the issues surrounding the construction of individuality. Further, it relies heavily on validating its findings by an appeal to objectivity and scientific rigour. The active nature of psychology, in that it actually deals with people and attempts to help and mould them, makes it a particularly profitable area for study, saliently highlighting the practical results of employing a dichotomizing knife to the individual and society.

Areas that this work does not have space to examine also need to be identified. Throughout, certain guiding assumptions concerning the philosophy of science, namely that it is a subjective and socially constructed form of knowledge, are taken as given. As the arguments supporting this position constitute a whole branch of philosophy in themselves, a detailed consideration of this position cannot be provided here.[5] The links between the philosophy of the Enlightenment, the status of scientific knowledge and capitalist economic formulations are also not evaluated fully. This is a subject that has been exhaustively covered by many theorists,[6] and space does not allow a full examination of these links and continuities. What this work will demonstrate is that individualism rests on a specific theory of human nature which leads to many of the conceptual problems encountered in social theory, namely conceiving of the individual and society as two separate entities and the implications of this separation.

A note on terminology needs to be introduced here so as to clarify the uses that certain key terms are to fulfil. Throughout the book I have used the terms "the individual" and "the subject" synonymously to relate to a person or member of the human species however constituted or conceived. No preconceptions as to the formulation, status or placement of this entity are implied by the terminology. In the last chapter of the book I employ the term "subjectivity". This is defined (echoing the postmodernism debate) as a theory of the subject which incorporates the following premise: the subject is always a positioned one that constitutes and is constituted by the multiple discourses that operate in society. Hence, the use of the term subjectivity does incorporate a performative theory of the subject.

The outline of the book is as follows: Chapter One sets the conceptual framework, showing how the debate between individualists and holists concerning the scope of social explanation is governed by traditionally entrenched approaches to what human nature is, and therefore is incapable of resolution within its current formulation. The chapter goes on to consider critics of individualism, one mounted by Lukes and a feminist analysis of individualism that finds fault with its inherent theory of human nature, arguing that these critiques neither strike at the heart of individualism nor sufficiently problematize its theory of human nature.

Chapter Two will consider in further detail the limitations of the collectivist approach which attempts to overcome individualism by considering society instead of the individual. The flaws in this approach will be evaluated by examining the recent techniques that have tried to overcome this dichotomy by theorizing the social constituents of the subject within social theory and social psychology. In this chapter particular attention will be paid to the difficulties these projects encounter, due to their implicit retention of separate notions of the individual and society.

Chapter Three locates the formulation of the subject under discussion in its historical context and goes on to illustrate the effects this subject has had for the devising of concepts such as prejudice and its translation into medical policy.

The final chapter concludes with a brief survey of ways to transcend the individual-society dichotomy by considering alternative theories of the subject. This involves an examination of the work of Foucault and Krishnamurti two theorists who, from radically different backgrounds, have nevertheless attempted to supplant the abstract subject for one that is more deeply enmeshed in social practices and thus can incorporate a dynamic relationship with society. The book concludes with a brief treatment of new paradigms and touches on different approaches in conceptualizing society and social relations.

While it is recognized that there may be conceptual flaws and problems raised by the discussion, I hope the general point that philosophical theories can and do have widespread practical and political importance is one that strikes home. Philosophy is increasingly demonstrating its value to the world outside the academy and it is only in this century that anything different has been supposed.

# Notes

1.  For a detailed discussion of the various forms of individualism see: Lukes,S. (1985), *Individualism*, Basil Blackwell, Oxford.

2.  See: Hayek,F.A. (1952), *The Counter Revolution of Science*, Glencoe, Ill. Hayek. (1949), *Individualism & the Economic Order,* London. Popper,K.R. (1977), *The Open Society & its Enemies*, Vol.1&2, Routledge & Kegan Paul, London. Popper. (1979), *The Poverty of Historicism,* Routledge & Kegan Paul, London. Ryan,A. (1984), *The Philosophy of the Social Sciences,* Macmillan, London.

3.  See footnote 2.

4.  This paradigm shift is articulated by many authors, particularly: Capra,F. (1987), *The Turning Point,* Flamingo, London. Laszlo,E.(1972), *Introduction to Systems Philosophy,* Gordon & Breach, London. These works provide a good introduction to the topic.

5.  See: Lakatos,I. & Musgrave,A. (1970), (ed.), *Criticism and the Growth of Knowledge*, Cambridge University Press. Kuhn,T.S. (1970), *The Structure of Scientific Revolutions*, University of Chicago Press.

6.  See: Capra (1987), op cit. And Hill,C. (1975), *The World Turned Upside Down: Radical ideas during the English Revolution,* Pelican, Harmondsworth.

# 1 The conceptual framework

## Introduction

The traditional argument between the individualists and the holists concerning the scope of social explanation is governed by entrenched approaches on both sides and this conceptual legacy, bequeathed to social science by the Enlightenment, leads to an impasse in the debate. In this chapter the limitations of formulating the debate in this traditional way are discussed, (namely, concentrating on the ontological and epistemological status of the two terms individual and society), arguing that this approach leads to stalemate with neither side capable of conceding or even recognizing the other's terms of analysis.[1] This is followed by an analysis of the criticisms levelled at individualism that address its inherent theory of human nature. Within the field of feminist scholarship theories of human nature that underlie social doctrines are of primary concern. The debate over what constitutes woman's nature, whether it is an innate, essential property or a socially conditioned subjectivity has been one of the main areas of study for feminist scholarship. This debate is not only of theoretical importance but has a practical dimension; namely, assessing and instigating liberatory political strategies. Hence, very interesting feminist critiques have been produced on this hitherto neglected area. This chapter looks at one example of such a feminist project, taking this as representative of critiques that have focused on the ideological and contingent nature of individualism. It will be argued that progress can be achieved by means of an examination of this debate because it begins to challenge the notion of universalist theories of humanity and locates human nature in a culturally specific context. However, this debate does not extend the critique far enough to fully eradicate the individual-society dichotomy and it is contended that neither the reformulation of the traditional debate nor this feminist analysis adequately overcome these conceptual problems and a more far reaching critique is needed to provide a new basis for analysis.

Discussions over the correct terminology with which to explain social phenomena have been long, convoluted and arduous, spanning many decades and philosophical positions. As Bacon is reported to have said, "the ill and unfit choice of words wonderfully obstructs the understanding." The discussion has concentrated upon two issues. The first involves the correct level at which social phenomena should be analysed; whether one should begin with the individual and work up to an explanation of the social, or start with social wholes and from these constructs determine individual behaviour. This is, in essence, the debate between holistic and individualistic explanations of human action and motivation. The second issue is concerned with the question of whether social phenomena are amenable to the same methods as natural science.

The very terms of the debate have set the conceptual lines along which it has run. The rival explanations have left us with a choice between putting the causational emphasis on either the individual or society. This entails choosing between two components of a fundamental dualism and neither type of explanation, in terms of the individual or a holistic analysis, has been successful in gaining precedent over the other. The fundamental problem, it would appear, may be due to the very presentation of the issues in such a framework.[2]

There is a basic problem inherent in this tendency to explain cultural phenomena as either manifestations of the acts of individuals or wholly in terms of social structures and consequently, within its own terms, the dispute has continued unabated. However, this chapter does not consider this dispute in detail; it addresses the very supposition that explanation has to lie in one domain or the other. The underlying reason why these two domains have become polarized can be found in the theories of human nature which underpin both collectivist and individualist doctrines. Both hold rival conceptions of what it is to be human, what motivates and influences human actions, what characterizes and differentiates humans from other animals and what constitutes a moral person. It is almost as if the two sets of theorists are talking about completely different subjects; one appears to be discussing an abstract individual untarnished by surrounding factors, and the other is discussing an environmentally conditioned creature which changes its characteristics as it changes cultures. It is these conflicting notions of the subject that inhibit the discussion of social phenomena and result in the answer being formulated exclusively in one set of terms or another. The possibility of a synthesis is ruled out by the basic presuppositions concerning the essential characteristics of human nature.

# The Traditional Debate

The opposition between the individualists and the holists can be reduced to the following questions. On which side of the individual-society dichotomy does the explanation of social phenomena lie? Should explanation be located at the level of the individual or can it be revealed by an analysis of society? The individualists locate explanation at the level of the individual; the holists locate it at the level of society.

## *The Individualist's Position*

According to A Quinton, who argues for the location of explanation at an individual level:

> If every statement about a social object is equivalent to, and can be replaced by a statement in which the predicates, whether the same or different as in the original statement, are predicates of individuals, then it rather trivially follows that every law is about individuals since it must implicitly be such a law itself. (Quinton, 1975-6:23)

In this way all social phenomena must be reduced to their component parts to render them intelligible.

This in essence is the position expounded by the doctrine of methodological individualism. All attempts to explain social phenomena and social wholes should only be couched in terms of facts about individuals. There can be statements formulated in social terms, but these have to be rejected as they cannot constitute "rock-bottom" explanations - they will only be the first stage in the process of elucidation, not the final explanation because a social construct can always be reducible to statements about individuals. As J W N Watkins puts it:

> There may be unfinished or half-way explanations of large-scale social phenomena (say full employment); but we shall not have arrived at rock-bottom explanations of such large scale phenomena until we have deduced an account of them from statements about the dispositions, beliefs, resources and inter-relations of individuals. (Watkins, 1959:505)

To look at social wholes is simply an inadequate method of analysis and one not capable of producing the real cause or explanation of any phenomena.

Methodological individualism is essentially a theory about the scope of social explanation and what counts as an adequate analysis of human action. Such an explanation can take a variety of forms, as it relates to various situations in which individuals might find themselves.

15

Looking at these situations ranging from the specifically personal to the distinctly social, it can be shown how methodological individualism explains actions by reducing them to individual terms devoid of any collective constructs.

Genetic make-up and brain states can be described in terms of human beings *qua* material objects. There is no reference made to the social situation, only the particular brain state or the unique consciousness is considered, the individual is seen as a mass of physiological impulses and studied accordingly. Moving on to the less personal states such as emotion (aggression or love for instance), these are described in relation to the individual's consciousness, seeing them as instinctive products, not products of their social surroundings or conditioned responses. This instinctive formulation of human action is what forms the basis of Hobbesian man, a man who acts on the basis of his innately determined characteristics. Under Hobbes' account society was seen as a mechanism to regulate the inevitable features of human nature. These features were, in essence, selfishness, competitiveness and an overriding desire for glory and power. For Hobbes man's dominant motivation was to attain power: "All passions may be reduced to the Desire of Power." Man did not want to co-operate but simply strove to gain power. Consequently, the natural state was one of war, in Hobbes' words, "every man against every man." Therefore men had to be forced, in the interests of survival, to co-operate with one another and live communally. Some followers of Hobbes viewed this state of affairs as inevitable because it was all encoded in human biology and hence unchangeable. In this way these instinctual entities are formed without recourse to the social setting of the person experiencing these emotions. They are traits that apply only to the individual and thus can be understood solely by examining that individual.

Finally, propositions involving terms such as war, voting and population growth, that seem necessarily to involve some notion of the social in order to fully appreciate them, can only be studied by reference to the effects that they can have on a particular person. Under the individualist analysis holistic terms such as class do not exist independently of individuals and can only be understood by examining the people that manifest them. It is neither necessary nor productive to look at cultural phenomena as a whole because this will be merely an amalgam of the actions of many individuals; the root cause of such phenomena will lie with the specific behaviour and aims of the individual component parts. Such a doctrine incorporates two implicit assumptions: reductionism (which embraces the belief that social facts must be reducible to those about individuals if they are to make any sense and therefore be capable of verification); and, that the methodology employed by natural science is diametrically opposed to that of social science, hence resulting in an incompatibility of method between the two disciplines. These two assumptions are inextricably linked and this point will be developed in the ensuing discussion. This discussion will aim to show how a traditional view of scientific objectivity enables social science to be seen as a subjective discipline that needs to ground itself in a reductionist methodology to make its findings intelligible.

The reductionist assumption is an integral part of the conceptual framework of individualism, J W N Watkins (1973) puts forward two arguments in support of this methodology. First, social things are created by personal attributes and thus any explanation of their composition must be accomplished by looking at the individuals who formed them. Second, a social scientist has no direct access to the overall structure of social wholes, because this is too vast an area to be studied comprehensively, and consequently can only derive reliable opinions about the dispositions and situations of individuals;[3] the individual is the only unit that can be realistically studied. This is where the chief distinction between natural and social sciences becomes apparent. The two sciences have a different subject matter, natural science studies phenomena amenable to objective inquiry, whereas social science incorporates the person both as the investigator and the object under study which is amenable only to subjective analysis. Due to these factors social science must employ a different methodology from that of natural science and be content with a different epistemological status for its findings. Social scientists must recognize that they can never achieve an objective status for their results in the same way as natural scientists can because the person under study is not an objective entity in the same way that the phenomena with which natural science concerns itself can be said to be. Hence, the fundamental difference between the two disciplines can be reduced to their respective objectivity and subjectivity.

From the concepts upon which individualism is based it is easy to see how the individualistic analysis will progress. By taking the individual as a starting point, it is necessary to utilize a compositive method when determining social phenomena. This method starts from simple elements and reproduces complex cultural structures by mental reconstruction, starting from the individual and deducing properties and regularities from its actions. These properties and regularities then become the basis for constructing a holistic concept. This is based on the assumption that social wholes, such as society or political movements, are not entities in their own right but amalgams of the actions and aims of many individuals. Any explanation of these phenomena must begin with an analysis of the individuals that make them up or one will fall into the trap of: "Mistaking for facts what are no more than provisional theories, models constructed by the popular mind to explain the connection between some of the individual phenomena which we observe." (Hayek, 1973:45) This is Hayek's version of the fallacy of misplaced concreteness. Under this analysis, the crucial point is that there can be no real knowledge of social wholes as no one person can fully appreciate the complexities of such a whole. Consequently, in order to give an adequate explanation of any facet of humanity it must be directed at a level where adequate knowledge can be reaped.

17

An explanation containing social wholes would explain phenomena in terms that did not actually exist and of which we could have no actual knowledge unless, of course, they were related to specific individuals. It is only possible to talk in terms of collective entities if they are used in a special sense, namely, as an amalgamation of the behaviour of individuals. These collective wholes do not stand for specific entities, as do individual terms, and have to be treated accordingly. A social term such as "the unemployed" can only be used in the wider sense to make generalizations. Any detailed explanation would have to deal specifically with the unemployed individuals themselves.

An important consequence of this methodology is that the two terms become incapable of any form of amalgamation if individuals and societies are depicted as two opposing entities, each with a different ontological and epistemological status. Indeed, for the individualist society does not exist in any meaningful way, as Mrs Thatcher said, "there is no such thing as society". The individual and society are treated as distinct and opposing entities and it is necessary to consider why this is so in further detail. The two terms are conceptualized as polarities for the following reasons. First, ontologically, it is argued that any propositions stated in terms of "societal facts" could not have any existence of their own without the individuals who think and act in certain ways. Thus statements about individuals are ontologically prior to those about "societal facts" and therefore have a primary existence. Propositions containing social constructs are relegated to a secondary level of existence and they are conceived as the sum of their individual parts. Hence, social wholes should be present only at the beginnings of the explanatory process or the depth of such an explanation would remain at a superficial level simply describing appearances rather than the root cause.

Second, epistemologically the two terms are again assigned to different categories. It is impossible to have the same kind of knowledge about society that one can have about the individual. "Societal facts" are not capable of being pointed to in the same way as material objects, each is only a series of interpersonal actions which can be highlighted when we wish to examine any fact concerning societal organization.[4] "Societal facts" are compound concepts made up of individual actions and consequently we can only have knowledge of them in so far as we can have knowledge about individuals. There can be knowledge of material objects (the subject matter of natural science) as they can be pointed to with some objective certainty, but there cannot be knowledge in the true sense of the word about the social sciences since it is essentially opinion, as Hayek argues: "Not opinion of the student of social phenomena of course, but opinion of those whose actions produce his object." Therefore one has to adopt a procedure: "Based on the experience that other people as a rule (though not always - e.g not if they are colour blind or mad) classify their sense impressions as we do." (Hayek,1973:30 & 28) Hayek elaborates this point in his work *The Sensory Order: An inquiry into the foundations of theoretical psychology*:

This does not mean that we may not be able in a different sense to "explain" particular mental events: it merely means that the type of explanation at which we aim in the physical sciences is not applicable to mental events. We can still use our direct ("introspective") knowledge of mental events in order to "understand", and in some measure even to predict, the results to which mental processes will lead in certain conditions. But this introspective psychology, the part of psychology which lies on the other side of the great cleavage which divides it from the physical sciences, will always have to take our direct knowledge of the human mind for its starting point. It will derive its statements about some mental processes from its knowledge about other mental processes, but it will never be able to bridge the gap between the realm of the mental and the realm of the physical. (Hayek,1987:192)

For Hayek the facts of social science are opinions which are rescued from being completely hidden because the object of study, allegedly, has a mind similar to the investigator. In this way "societal facts" fall between two stools: they cannot be known in the same way as material objects and they cannot be known in the same way as individual actions. Hence, social institutions cannot be analysed without knowledge of the intentions and purposes of the individuals who use them. On this reading it would seem that epistemologically "societal facts" have no status at all in the sense that they cannot be known in their own right without recourse to the individuals who make them up.[5]

As a result of conceptualizing the terms "individual" and "society" as ontologically and epistemologically distinct the debate becomes crystallized with the theorists in rival camps. Watkins sums up this incommensurability: "Just as mechanism is contrasted with the organicist idea of physical fields, so methodological individualism is contrasted with sociological holism or organicism." He then goes on to say that: "If methodological individualism means that human beings are supposed to be the only moving agents in history, and if sociological holism means that some superhuman agents or factors are supposed to be at work in history, then these two alternatives are exhaustive." (Watkins,1959:505)

Thus the debate has become formulated in terms of twin antagonisms, with each set of protagonists incorporating into their analysis assumptions that often go unclarified and unjustified, leading to a fundamental intractability between the rival theorists. The holists have often constructed their analysis more as a defensive response to individualism than as an inherently viable theory and it is their account that will now be considered.

## Responses to Individualism

The opponents of individualism [6] have argued against this position by contending that the nexus of causation should lie with society, keeping the outline of the debate intact and concentrating their attack upon issues such as reductionism and the ontological and epistemological status of social constructs. One example of this type of analysis is Mandelbaum's argument concerning the ontological status of social wholes. He contends that the ontological claim that, "societal facts" could not have any existence of their own without individuals who think and act in certain ways, does not lead to the conclusion that is thought to follow from it. "One need not hold that society is an entity independent of all human beings in order to hold that societal facts are not reducible to the facts of individual behaviour." (Mandelbaum, 1973:230)

In this way Mandelbaum attempts to overcome the individualist's claims by putting forward the following argument: as people are influenced by the society they are in, so the facts which concern the nature of society must in some respect be independent of them. In order to be influenced by a factor it must have some separate existence, as societally-orientated behaviour is conditioned by an already existing set of "societal facts". The individualist, however, might still ask what ontological status these "societal facts" have if they are dependent for their existence on individuals, although not identical with them. Mandelbaum argues that their ontological status can still be postulated, and uses the example of a traditional epiphenomenalist, who would regard as similar the relationship between brain events and the contents of consciousness, namely, conciousness is postulated as a derivation of brain activity.

If there are reasons for asserting that the content of consciousness is different from brain states and that although consciousness does depend on the latter, it is not identical or non-existent, then these facts cannot be rejected because of some prior ontological commitment. As Mandelbaum puts it:

> Just as I have claimed that the component parts of a society are the elements of its organisation and are not the individuals without whom it would not exist, so the epiphenomenalist would (I assume) say that the parts of the individual's field of consciousness are to be found within specific data of consciousness and not in the brain events upon which consciousness depends. (Mandelbaum, 1973:232)

Consequently, the premise that "societal facts" depend upon the existence of people does not preclude the contention that these facts are irreducible to those solely concerning individuals.

The debate is frequently couched in terms which only one set of protagonists would be likely to agree on - a situation which is due to its formulation in terms of two conflicting entities (the individual and society). The critics of individualism continue with detailed

20

refutations of both the principle of reductionism [7] and the contention that it is impossible to procure knowledge of "societal facts" as well as knowledge of individuals. The opposite opinion is stated in Hayek's formulation of social knowledge: "There is no other way toward an understanding of social phenomena but through our understanding of individual actions directed toward other people guided by their expected behaviour." (Hayek,1949:6)

This view of the very epistemological status of "societal facts" would be hotly contested by Mandelbaum, who would differentiate such "societal facts" from the level of personal introspection and assign to them a more concrete and objective status. He argues that any objection to the existence of such facts, which presents them only as a series of interpersonal actions (and therefore not capable of being pointed to in the same sense as material objects), would lead to a bizarre theory of knowledge. A theory which contends that all empirically meaningful concepts must be ultimately reducible to data which can be directly inspected will lead one to assert that the reducibility of "societal facts" is inevitable. However, Mandelbaum argues that this position is untenable, as a proof that it cannot account for our apprehension of an individual's actions is enough to refute the epistemological support for reductionism. The individualist would argue that it is not possible to understand a person's behaviour if it is not directly apparent to the senses, unless their intention is known. But this contention would severely reduce what is classed as knowledge and commit the individualist to a strict form of empiricism. Unless we only have understanding because of our experiences, which would appear to be unwarranted, it must be acknowledged that we can understand aspects of behaviour that are not directly apparent to our senses, as indeed Hayek recognizes when he contends that the subject base for social sciences is the opinions of the object under study which we classify by a rationalist procedure. [8] Therefore, what counts as knowledge must be widened and this widening of knowledge admits factors the reductionists are attempting to deny, namely that one can use individual facts as a basis for knowledge of "societal facts". In this context the genetic fallacy must be avoided, as Mandelbaum recognizes: "The origin of our knowledge is not identical with the knowledge itself." (Mandelbaum,1973:233) So it must be conceded that we can understand aspects of behaviour that are not directly apparent to our senses, otherwise we would have such a limited understanding of the world as to make general comprehensions and statements impossible - a situation which is clearly not the case.

It is at this point that the debate over the status of "societal facts" reaches a position of stalemate, with each protagonist holding a different epistemological theory. This leads to vastly different conclusions about whether these social wholes can be said to exist at all and the level on which they can be examined. These are the lines along which the traditional debate has run, with the possibility of either position gaining ascendancy very unlikely. What this debate rarely considers is the theories of human nature upon which these doctrines are based

21

and it is the existence of such unsupported assumptions that clouds the debate. It is to this issue that the next section will turn.

## The Theory Within

It will be argued that it is the different theories of human nature upon which individualism and collectivism are based that leads to their mutual incomprehension. What holds methodological individualism together as a doctrine is the theory of human nature on which it rests and this can be characterized as the notion of an abstract individual. It is this implicit assumption about human nature that leads to the stalemate between the opposing camps of holism and individualism. Any doctrine of individualism has to be based on this formulation of the subject or its arguments as to the reducibility of "societal facts" become meaningless. It will also be argued that the holists themselves incorporate into their theorizing a less extreme form of the abstract individual but one that includes a notion of the subject as a pre-given entity nonetheless (this issue is discussed in greater detail in the following chapter).

This notion of the abstract individual is summed up by L Dumont:

> For the moderns, under the influence of Christian and Stoic individualism, natural law, as opposed to positive law, does not involve social beings but individuals, ie, men each of whom is self-sufficient, as made in the image of God and as the repository of reason. This is to say that, in the idea of jurists in the first place, first principles regarding the constitution of the State (and of society) have to be extracted or deduced, from the inherent properties or qualities of man taken as an autonomous being independently of any social or political attachment. The state of nature is the state, logically prior to social and political life, in which only individual man is considered, logical priority blending into historical authority, the state of nature is the state in which men are supposed to have lived before the foundation of society or state. (Dumont,1965:29-30)

Here, the expression "man" is taken to be an independent entity existing in a contextless state, pursuing the same motives in whatever society he is placed. As a consequence of the initial premise that humans influence, create and delimit society and that this is the root cause of the formation of such a society, it is inferred that human nature exists independently of this given social context and can be characterized without reference to its social setting. It becomes reasonable to assume that society can be defined as an artifice, a way of furthering independently-given individual objectives and not as an entity in its own right. Society will play some part in influencing the individual participants, but ultimately, as S Lukes states: "This giveness of fixed and invariant human psychological features leads to an abstract conception of the individual who is seen as merely the bearer of those features, which

22

determine his behaviour, and specify his interests, needs and rights."(Lukes,1985:73)

Most modern theorists would not wish to advance such an extreme notion of human nature as Natural Law theorists such as Hobbes, Rousseau and Kant held; they would allow the thesis that society does exert some influence on the subject and recognize that a position which completely disregards environmental factors is untenable. Even so, the crucial point is still not lost, namely, that as the subject has basic, inherent, pre-given qualities, the analysis of causation must always run from the individual upwards. Society has to be explained by reference to its individual components and, once the direction of causation is set, it is very difficult to talk of societies influencing the individual. This has become precluded by the notion of the abstract individual and is implicitly asserted in Hayek's thought when he talks of psychological states being the correct area in which to locate the nexus of causation.

Now, if it is recognized that this notion of the subject is implicit in the theory of methodological individualism, it is possible to see how the holist-individualist debate is unsolvable in its present formulation. If one takes this abstract subject as the starting point for the theory, it is impossible to come to any other conclusions than those reached by the individualists. If the subject is basically a discrete entity with only subsidiary influences from environmental factors, then it will necessarily follow that society is just an amalgam of all these individual wants and aims. Thus, social wholes have to be reducible to the location of the individual or a nonsensical situation will arise, in which "societal facts" could not tell us anything of importance about the way we live, except as once-removed abstractions, simply generalizations generated from an amalgam of individual intentions.

All the basic tenets of methodological individualism follow from this conception of its subject and lead to the important conceptual splits as far as methodology is concerned. Hayek, for example, argues that it is only possible to speak of social wholes in a special sense once they have been constructed out of the behaviour of individuals. This leads him straight into a form of systematic subjectivism; that all knowledge in the social sciences is essentially opinion, opinion of the subject under study. It is this subjectivism that characterizes the main difference between natural and social sciences. The natural sciences are deemed to be concerned with objective facts and consequently employ a different method from that of the social sciences. For Hayek, values and opinions are the correct area of study for social science, based on the understanding that the object of study has a mind similar to our own and hence only subjective knowledge can be procured.

> From the fact that we shall never be able to achieve more that an "explanation of the principle" by which the order of mental events is determined, it also follows that we shall never achieve a complete "unification" of all sciences in the sense that all phenomena of which it treats can be described in physical terms. In the study of human

action, in particular, our starting point will always have to be our direct knowledge of the different kinds of mental events, which to us must remain irreducible entities. (Hayek,1987:191)

If such a notion of the subject were rejected, it would be impossible to employ this method fruitfully. For, if an element of social conditioning were allowed into the formulation of human nature, then the notion that the subject under study has a mind similar to our own could be contentious. Due to this social conditioning, minds might be radically different in different contexts, and thus Hayek's methodology would become meaningless. Minds need not be similar if they are culturally conditioned; for minds to be similar in all contexts an abstract construction of the subject is needed. A reverse method would have to be reinstated if the notion of the subject was transformed into one which incorporated the idea of society influencing the individual, a method in which society is seen as the locus of causation and the individual viewed as the product of that society.

There have been various critiques of individualism that address this inherent theory of human nature and these will be considered below. It is a relatively new departure to bring the underlying theories of human nature into the debate over the acceptability of individualism. The question of concern is one of the precise relationship between this abstract unitary theory of human nature and the doctrine of individualism itself. Are the two integral to each other or can they be separated and individualism enjoy coherence as a theory without incorporating this construction of human nature? The two critiques considered here give different answers to this question and their theorizing provides a greater understanding of the nature of this relationship.

## The Emergence of a Critique

### Lukes' Reformulation of Individualism

Most theorists do not acknowledge that it is the conflict over how one defines human nature that leads to the stalemate in the debate. Lukes, in his book *Individualism*, goes some way to recognizing this when he highlights the links between the various formulations of individualism and liberal democracy. He then goes on to examine how the notion of the abstract individual affects the core values of individualism, equality and liberty. These will be considered along with his criticism of the very notion of abstract individualism.

Lukes argues that classical liberal democratic theory depends on an abstract conception of the individual to validate its notion of a good society. As Lukes states, the concept of the abstract individual is essential to any form of political individualism, "from Locke to the present day, which, as we have suggested, all presuppose a picture of civil society, whose members are "independent centres of consciousness" and have

24

given, non-context-dependent interests, wants, motives, purposes, [and] needs, etc." Due to people's essential nature and their ultimate autonomy: "The authority of government rests on the citizens' independently-given consent, represents individual interests, and protects their freedom or rights to pursue their interests." (Lukes,1985:138) The liberal conception of society as the amalgam of many individuals all following their own ends, with the function of government being merely to adjudicate between rival claims when the situation arises, builds on this abstract conception of the individual. Lukes quotes Macpherson on the basis of liberal society when he says, "the core of Locke's individualism is the assertion that every man is naturally the sole proprietor of his own person and capacities - the absolute proprietor in that he owes nothing to society for them - and especially the absolute proprietor of his capacity to labour."(Lukes,1985:139) Lukes sums up this formulation of individualism within liberalism, by saying: "The idea of the independent, rational citizen is a central presupposition of classical liberal democratic theory."(1985:139)

After establishing the links between individualism and liberalism, and arguing that it necessitates certain social relations, namely a classical liberal democracy, Lukes goes on to take issue with the concept of abstract individualism, finding it an inadequate explanation of human nature, "it contradicts all the accumulated lessons of sociology and social anthropology and of social psychology."(1985:151) His interest lies in saving the core doctrines of individualism from being thrown out with the rejection of this theory of human nature. After reviewing the various facets of individualism, Lukes concludes with the argument that it is possible to keep the essential core of individualism - namely, the notion of individual autonomy, respect for individual rights, and the subsequent implications for equality and liberty - and reject the conception of the abstract individual, that, "runs like a connecting thread through the various forms of political individualism."(1985:138)

Lukes defines these core values in the following way: "I conclude that equality is centrally based on human respect, and that liberty is an amalgam of personal autonomy, lack of public interference and the power of self-development." (1985:131). He sees no logical connection between the notion of the abstract individual and other core ideas of individualism. "Nor does a commitment to equality and liberty, as we have analysed them, logically imply the acceptance of individualist political, economic or religious doctrines." (1985:147) Lukes states that an adherence to methodological individualism in no way implies that one is any more likely to respect or ensure self-development of an individual than if one was committed to the existence of social wholes. He then puts forward a stronger thesis, "that the only way to realize the values of individualism is through a humane form of socialism."(1985:157)

In criticizing the abstract individual, and attempting to rid individualism of this archaic notion of human beings, Lukes recognizes that methodological individualism is founded on a specific theory of human nature, and one that is open to question rather than a timeless truth:

> I have argued that the abstract conception of the individual is doubly inadequate; first, because it in fact forms the basis for a particular ideological view of a certain sort of society and its social relations; and second, because it represents a primitive and a- or pre-sociological view of the nature of the individual. (1985:152)

Although the removal of abstract individualism from other forms of individualism would be a worthy project and could transmute them into more plausible theories, Lukes fails to see that the wider permutations of this theory of human nature (upon which individualism is based), do not only rest on a notion of an abstracted subject. The abstract individual is the extreme form, the untainted man at his starkest. Lukes' critique of this is well-grounded, but he does not see that there are subtler versions at work that cannot be pulled away from the core of individualism as he hopes. Individualism in all its forms is based on a concept of the subject that is a unitary being, operating within a society that is a product of millions of like beings coming together. People create society, but society only creates people in a limited way. Lukes does not see that he is formulating values such as liberty, freedom and equality within a liberal framework, and one that he himself argues is built on this conception of the unitary individual. His "humane form of socialism" will never be possible if he retains these liberal values, as the unitary individual is inevitably carried within these formulations.

The formulation of the subject does not have to be one of stark, abstract individualism for socialist theory to flounder. It can admit that environmental factors could play a part in people's development, that it is not solely innately possessed characteristics that delimit our actions, and still retain the idea of an unitary, pre-given subject. There is also another facet of this subject that needs to be problematized, namely the whole idea of the individual (however constituted) at the centre of analysis and causation. To locate the individual in this position, a theory of human nature is required that essentially sees the person as a lone, discrete entity. A theory that gives priority to cultural influences would necessitate a different positioning for the individual in the explanation process.

This is where Lukes' analysis falls down; if the abstract individual or its weaker versions are taken from individualism as a whole, then the entire structure of analysis collapses. The positioning of causation has to change if there is no such entity as an independent unitary subject. If this is the case then analysis has to begin, and be largely concentrated, at the societal level and all the major premises of individualism - that social constructs must be reducible to those couched in individual terms and these terms must form the focus of consideration - have to fall by the wayside, thus ceasing to be a doctrine of individualism.

Lukes goes on to argue that what is needed to replace this concept of abstract individualism is a notion of the subject as a "person", which defines "person" as a human being with certain capacities. The way in which these capacities are developed is left open, for the individual is the shaper of its own destiny, rather than a subject with pre-given qualities that necessitate a predetermined future. In this way,

Respecting them as *persons*, in these ways, involves the kind of understanding of both their social and their individual aspects which the abstract view of them precludes. For, on the one hand, such respect requires us to take account of them as social selves - moulded and constituted by their societies - whose achievements of, and potential for, autonomy, whose valued activities and involvements and whose potentialities are, in large part, socially determined and specific to their particular social context. On the other hand, it requires us to see each of them as an actually or potentially autonomous centre of choice (rather than bundle composed of a certain range of wants, motives, purposes, interests, etc.), able to choose between, and on occasion transcend, socially-given activities and involvements, and to develop his or her respective potentialities in the available forms sanctioned by the culture - which is both a structural constraint and a determinant of individuality.(1985:149)

This redefining of the subject does not go far enough in overcoming the difficulties and unwelcome conclusions that he attributes to the doctrines of individualism (for instance a commitment to liberal bourgeois society), because one is still dealing with an individual at the centre of analysis and not society. He uses this formulation to argue for a concept of human nature that can be "modified in each historical epoch" and appreciates the social nature of man, in which society's influence will be given sufficient weight. On balance this reformulation is just a rehashing of the problem in a more palatable form. It does not alter the central place that the subject occupies in the analysis of social explanation, nor does it alter the notion of an abstract unitary individual; the term "person" is essentially analogous with this definition of individuality.

The fundamental problem that theorists such as Lukes fail to confront in their critique of individualism is an analysis of the extent to which such theories presuppose, are built upon, and have a reciprocal relationship with, certain conceptions of human nature. The formulation of the subject as an isolated, independent individual is inimical to a theory of human nature that sees people as being formed to a large extent by certain innate capacities, and only modified by environmental factors in a limited fashion. This formulation is necessitated by putting the individual into a distinct category in contrast to society. If the question is posed in these dualistic terms, certain paths of analysis are already mapped out before speculation has even begun. The polarization of the two terms precludes answers that contain any synthesis between the individual and society.

## The Feminist Critique

The problems created by this unitary abstract subject require further analysis and feminist thought has been one of the predominant areas that has attempted a critique of this implicit assumption of human nature within individualism. N Scheman's paper, "Individualism, and the Objects of Psychology", provides a good example of the direction such criticisms have taken and goes some way to highlighting the problems and issues raised in this debate by focussing on the implications these theories of human nature have for political and social arrangements. She too is concerned with the relationship between the doctrine of individualism and the abstract, unitary theory of human nature, but comes to a different conclusion about the nature of the relationship from that of Lukes. Scheman argues that the two are inseparable, as individualism is based on this theory of human nature and any attempt to revise it would result in a rebuttal of individualism itself.

Scheman's critique is centred upon the notion of what she calls individualism in the philosophy of mind which puts forward the contention that our psychological states must be analysed as a purely individual phenomena and not linked to the cultural context of the person. [9] This position, she contends, is seldom explicitly stated or supported: "What there are no arguments for to the best of my knowledge, is the underlying assumption that, whatever there may be, psychological states can be assigned and theorized about on an individual basis."(Scheman,1983:225) She attacks the implicit assumptions of psychology on similar grounds to Shotter (see Chapter Two) by contending that psychology incorporates emotive statements under the guise of objective scientific truths. She then goes on to argue that this individualism in the philosophy of mind has ramifications for feminism because it perpetuates patriarchal family arrangements, by instilling such an ideology in children from an early age. [10] Grimshaw sums this up by saying:

> Scheman takes as her starting point the account given by Chodorow and others...of the development of boys and girls in the situation where early primary care is undertaken by women. She argues that the stress on separation and difference from others which Chodorow's theory sees as characterizing the masculine psyche can be connected to the doctrine of "individualism" in psychology, and to political liberalism. (Grimshaw,1986:167)

To consider Scheman's position in more detail; first her account of individualism in psychology is analysed and then the implications this has for liberal political theory is developed. Second, her account of patriarchal child-rearing practices is elucidated.

The underlying assumption in philosophical accounts of the objects of psychology is that psychological states apply to us singly and this is due to several assumptions that are never explicitly considered or supported. The first assumption is what Scheman calls a straightforward theoretical demand, and the second, a common sense view. The former assumption is necessitated by the physiological premises that such an analysis is built on, namely, that as particular states of individuals are seen as physiological objects, physiology needs to ascribe these states to us singly. If one sees these states of individuals, such as emotions and beliefs, as simply physiological objects reducible to the mechanical operations and nerve impulses of a brain, then one has to couch the analysis of these states in individual terms rather than at a more public and universal level. The common sense assumption is accordingly an ontological one, namely that individuals are prior to and more important in the analysis of causation than social wholes.

These premises are based on the principle of reductionism mentioned earlier: when a person displays emotions, ultimately their causation has to be said to lie in the functionings of their own minds and it is possible to reduce any statement about social wholes to its individual component parts. This is an untenable position according to Scheman, psychological states cannot be understood as operating like simple urges that may occur or not, but they must be viewed in their social context. As she puts it:

> We can, I think, maintain that our twinges, pangs and so on are particular events no matter what our social situation, but it does not follow that the same is true for more complex psychological objects, such as emotions, beliefs, motives, and capacities. What we need to know in order to identify them is how to group together introspective states and behaviour and how to interpret it all. The question is one of meaning, not just at the level of what to call it but at the level of there being an "it" at all. And questions of meaning and interpretation cannot be answered in abstraction from a social setting. (1983:229)

This position links Scheman to a tradition in the philosophy of mind, akin to Wittgenstein, that sees states of mind as incapable of explanation if viewed as arising from a sort of introspective object. [11] Grimshaw makes the point: "Scheman engages with a tradition in the philosophy of mind which argues that the way in which we learn concepts such as "anger" or "remorse" or "pain" cannot be understood as arising merely from a sort of "inner pointing" to some introspectible object."(Grimshaw,1986:163) In this way there must be public criteria for the meaning of language.

Scheman's argument highlights certain prior commitments and philosophical underpinnings of individualism in the philosophy of mind, which are, first, a commitment to physicalism which will reduce any psychological states to the functionings of one mind. She criticizes this notion on the grounds that it is impossible to provide an adequate analysis of meaning for psychological states if they are seen as attaching to us singly. The second commitment is, "an appeal to (philosophically coloured) common sense" (1983:227) that views individuals as ontologically prior to, and hence more important than, social wholes in an analysis of causation. This is a reductionist position and one she finds untenable.

There is not sufficient space to evaluate Scheman's analysis of these prior commitments in the philosophy of mind or elaborate the case against reductionism (the issue of reductionism was discussed earlier in this chapter). She argues these are reasons that might be offered for thinking that individualist assumptions are true. Whereas, her arguments concerning how these ideas and constructs have been perpetuated are of more relevance to the issues in hand and represent Scheman's distinctive approach to the debate. Therefore, her analysis of why these individualistic assumptions in the philosophy of mind have had such a persuasive hold will be examined in preference to concentrating on her explanation of why the universality of individualist assumptions are so prevalent, which she puts down to physicalism and reductionism, two widely accepted concepts. In her words, "rather than purported justifications of the assumption, they are attempts at explaining how it has come to have the hold on us that it does."(1983:230) This is a consideration not usually addressed by critiques of individualism. Thus her contribution usefully focuses on the political and social consequences of holding a theory of individualism.

The reason Scheman gives for these individualistic premises being so deeply entrenched in our society is due to their operation as a type of ideology, forming a system of beliefs and value judgements that masquerade as the way things naturally are and have to be, rather than as prerogative concepts. The mechanisms by which these assumptions are perpetuated are, according to Scheman, two-fold; first, "the connections between the individualistic assumption in the philosophy of mind and the notion of the self embodied in the ideology of liberal individualism," and, second, the tying of the "notion of the self to the psychosexual development of males in a patriarchal culture where childcare is primarily in the hands of women."(1983:230)

The first mechanism for the perpetuation of individualistic assumptions in the philosophy of mind is the notion of the self embodied in the ideology of liberal individualism.

> To see the individualist assumption as stemming from the ideology of liberal individualism is to see that what purports to be a statement about how things naturally are is instead an expression of a historically specified way of structuring some set of social interactions. (1983:230-1)

Individualism gains credence by dressing itself in the mantle of undisputed fact.

It is this supposed naturalness of the claims of individualism that characterizes it as an ideology for Scheman - individualism posits certain culturally formulated traits as natural characteristics. In this way the experiencing of psychological states singly and personally becomes an inherent facet of humanity and will act as a constraining factor on any social theory, because it is necessary to respect these innate characteristics or founder on incompatibility. This psychological individualism forms the bedrock of liberal society. Building on an abstract individualist concept of the subject, classical liberal social theory examines means to entice or threaten such individuals into stable relationships with one another because, if left to their own devices, the solitary individual might have no need for society. Thus, society is conceived as an amalgam of all these individuals respecting the separateness of all people and providing mechanisms for judging the claims of one against another. At the same time it leaves the individual alone to be self-defining and incorporates a notion of negative rather than positive liberties.

Central to liberal political theory is an individualism of method, that everyone be counted as one and one only. It postulates that people should be treated in the same way and no definition of what constitutes the proper way to live should be laid down by the state. Everyone should be free to organize themselves as they wish. Of course, not all people can be treated equally and their freedom may be limited if it conflicts with the liberty of others. [12] This gives rise to a conflict over which freedoms to give precedence, legislating against pornography is an example of such a conflict in practice. Banning pornography is often opposed on the grounds that it would involve censorship and that this could be a dangerous precedent to set as it restricts certain people's freedom. This conflicts with women's freedom not to be confronted with offensive publications, illustrating a tension that has not been resolved, a problem of defining what harm is sufficient to justify limiting pornographers' liberty. This debate highlights important features in the way in which a liberal political system conceives and attempts to deal with social problems. In the censorship of pornography example the discussion becomes crystallized around issues such as the extent and level of harm produced by the possible actions, with each type of harm defined as that which can accrue to an individual (or possibly a collection of individuals). There is no room in the debate for a consideration of the structural and cultural facets that affect relationships between men and women. These culturally determined relationships have a bearing on how pornography is received by women (namely as offensive and threatening rather than as sexually titallating material). In this way, the harm to the pornographer cannot be balanced, I would argue, with the harm to an individual woman. In the liberal analysis each individual is considered as equal, and therefore should be treated equally, but women do not have an equal status in our society and therefore need more protection, legally, from the state. It is this defining of freedom in the negative sense that results in a blindness to the realities of inequalities.

31

Scheman then goes on to draw particular attention to problems that could arise for liberalism concerning its adherence to an individualism of substance. To be committed to an individualism of substance would rule out any organizational plans for a society that included communitarian arrangements. This could be an undesirable end for liberal political theorists,

> for two reasons: we may be required by facts about developmental psychology to see human beings as springing from, perhaps even necessarily continuing to see themselves as members of, particular social groups, and communitarian ideals may well be among the possible visions the state is committed to respecting equally. (1983:231)

In this way an adherence to an individualism of substance could be damaging to liberal theory, in that it could not take on board new developments.

This commitment to an individualism of substance may well have to be eliminated from liberal theory in order for it to be more tenable in the light of advancements in psychology and anthropology. However, even if this argument is accepted, it has to be questioned whether liberal political theory can function as persuasively as it has done so far without being committed to an abstract individualist conception of human nature. It might be possible to eliminate this theory of human nature from liberalism, but the effect this could have on the other major tenet of individualism - individualism of method - is questionable. Scheman considers whether it is possible to adhere to this individualism of method without being committed to an individualism of substance and deliberates over whether the two elements can be prised apart.

In answer to this question, Scheman cites J.Rawls' *A Theory of Justice* as an example of such a project, one that attempts to separate individualism of method from an individualism of substance. She asks whether classical liberalism can keep its basic methodological tenets and substitute a theory of human nature that incorporates the notion of socially constituted beings. She also questions whether classical liberalism, by basing itself on methodological individualism, has discriminated against communitarian ideas. "An alternative way of framing this concern is to ask whether in claiming neutrality among views of human nature...the state is in fact expressing some particular set of views to the exclusion of others." (1983:232) Scheman's answer to this question of the related nature of the two forms of individualism is that it is not possible to separate an individualism of method from an individualism of substance. The view of humans as socially constructed, with their mental states interpenetrable only in the context of a social setting, would seem incompatible with a social and political theory that sees society as built on the amalgamated aims of many separate individuals and treats them accordingly. It is impossible to prise the two apart, since liberal social theory is based on the acceptance of abstract individualism, the first follows logically from the second. Scheman argues that there is a fundamental incompatibility between liberalism and a socially constructed view of human nature:

> If this incompatibility is real (as I think it is) the liberal has good reasons to resist the view of the social construction of the objects of psychology: only if psychological states can be seen as attaching to individuals in abstraction from their social setting can we expect to appeal to them to justify forms of social organisation. (1983:232)

Hence, English liberalism is based on an empiricist epistemology which uses a certain formulation of the subject to justify both scientific and political theories. [13] Scheman calls the psychological theory that underpins individualism the psychological realist thesis; emotions and beliefs and so on are really there as particular states and therefore empirically verifiable. It would be impossible, Scheman argues, to take away this thesis from liberal individualism. The opposite of this thesis would be a non-realist individualism that would view psychological objects as constructs, ways of making sense of the world around us, rather than referring to any certain objects. This psychological realism thesis characterizes what has become the definition of the subject under liberalism, and to try and incorporate a non-realist thesis would be incompatible with liberal social arrangements.

In order for liberalism to retain consistency and define human nature in such a way that would cohere with its political organization, psychological states must remain independent of forms of social organization. A theory of human nature that views people as socially constituted would be incompatible with a political theory that conceives social wholes as comprising of an amalgam of independently existing characteristics of individuals.

What liberalism needs for its theory to remain consistent is something non-arbitrary to appeal to when talking about such psychological states, to prevent the whole debate from lapsing into hopeless subjectivity. Liberalism needs to build on the psychological realism thesis (that psychological states are definite particulars) or psychological states would be identifiable only by reference to the individual that possessed them, and be independent of any outside verification. This would result in an inability to evaluate rival claims or contentions. For liberalism, psychological states have to be definite particulars and exist within the individual, to cohere with liberal political and methodological theory. Scheman sums this up:

> The idea that psychological states are definite particulars is the natural mirror to the liberal conception of individuals....The more individualistic the theory the greater the need for psychological realism....I want to suggest that these connections account for some of the strength of psychological individualism: our liberal view of

persons as separable individuals would seem to require, or at least to fit most naturally with, a view of psychological objects as existing brutally in us. (1983:234)

It is in this way that liberal theory manages to receive largely unchallenged acceptance. The ideological formulation of the subject, according to Scheman, gives this notion of human nature a form of general applicability. It is argued that this conception of human nature is natural and correct, while in fact it is simply a political and cultural specific. It is a particular formulation of human nature which is necessary for the functioning of liberalism and it is an integral part of the doctrine of individualism. In this way an individualism of substance (individualism's abstract subject) and an individualism of method (liberalism) cannot be prised apart. The latter presupposes and builds on the former. Individualism builds logically on the notion of an abstract individual, and a theory of human nature incorporating the influence of society would result in the rejection of the fundamental claims of liberalism. [14] Hence, the liberal view of persons as separate individuals seems to require the notion of psychological objects existing solely in us.

Scheman's account makes a significant contribution to the exposure of the individualistic theories upon which liberalism builds, and the forging of links between psychological theories and the philosophy of mind is an important development. This analysis of the possible ideological nature of such theories and their connection with certain political doctrines makes explicit a relationship that has long been implicitly accepted.

Scheman then goes on to advance the second mechanism for the perpetuation of individualistic assumptions. "My reason for the widespread acceptance of the individualist assumption ties this view of the self to patriarchal child-rearing practices." (1983:234) These child-rearing practices result in adults who exemplify the individualistic view of the self, thus giving rise to the opinion that it is essentially a human and not an ideological construct. Scheman bases her account on the work of N Chodorow and D Dinnerstein, (1978 & 1976) who examine the consequences of child-rearing being largely in the hands of women. It is in this analysis of the problem that some of the tensions in her position are revealed.

Scheman uses the "object relations" theory, which sees the self as developing essentially in relation to a particular other. This theory provides the basis for an alternative explanation by looking at the structure of child-rearing practices that produce the individuals under question:

> I want to suggest that if certain recent accounts of gender differences in psychosexual development are correct, they would lead us to expect that precisely such an individualistic view of the

self would come to be both exemplified by men and taken by women alike as essentially human. (1983:234)

These child-rearing methods can be seen as producing men of whom these political and philosophical views seem factually descriptive, thus giving rise to the idea that these views are the result of what human nature actually is, rather than what is produced. The philosophy of the autonomous individual is a defensive ratification of the psychological development of men raised in patriarchal society rather than a natural exposition of human nature.

By being told that these psychical structures are universal, people are prevented from criticizing them and from considering alternatives based on conflicting experiences:

> This inter-relationship is characteristic of an ideology; a set of views purports to tell us the facts, what is "naturally" true, in the nature of things, and through doing this helps to structure social institutions in such a way as to produce people who tend to exemplify these views, thereby providing evidence for their own truth. (1983:235)

Under this analysis one explanation is given to show how the notion of the unitary individual is not a natural pre-given entity but is seen, instead, as one constructed within certain social contexts.

Scheman argues that within this social context people are conditioned to behave in a certain way and this exemplifies the concept of the abstract individual. People do not display these traits because they are naturally abstract individuals, they display them because they are products of their environment. Child-rearing practices determine the adult. These child-rearing practices are not inevitable responses to human need but have developed out of a certain economic and political situation. People brought up in this situation will become moulded in the image of the liberal conception of man, while women will view their condition as somehow unnatural because they will not fit into the dominant paradigm of what it is to be a rational member of the community. Such conceptions of rationality will be formed in a masculine framework. As people exhibit these traits it gives the individualist grounds for concluding that humans are inherently like this. This commits the naturalistic fallacy of mistaking an ought for an is.

From Scheman's analysis, it is possible to identify the tensions and limitations in her critique of individualism. It is open to criticism on the grounds that her concentration on the results of patriarchal child-rearing practices, as exemplified in the work of Chodorow and Dinnerstein, does not take into consideration or give equal weight to other factors that can influence the subject, such as schooling or the media. The mother is not the only contact the child has with the world, no matter how patriarchal the society may be. Any analysis that attempts to give primacy to one cause over and above all others is bound to result in the neglect or the trivialization of certain factors unless causation can be unproblematically associated with one factor. However, this is rarely the case. It is a methodology borrowed from the very individualism that Scheman criticises, a methodology which locates causation in one single area and negates the complexity of forces that can operate on the subject. This is a methodology that rules out the possibility of synthesis due to a framework that necessitates a unitary explanation, one that prioritizes causes instead of perceiving them as having equal and diverse effects.

The adherents of this explanation in terms of child-rearing practices can also be said to be guilty of an ahistorical analysis of the situation. Women, especially in less financially secure positions, have often gone out to work, providing children with a less than conventional role model. Scheman can be accused of mistaking individualism's ideological suppositions for reality. Many families do not conform to the conventional notion of the nuclear family. It is used just as much for the purposes of prescription as it is for description and can be regarded as something people should aspire to, a mechanism of control, rather than an unquestioned statement of fact. To argue that such child-rearing practices are a major factor in the prevalence of individualist assumptions is both a factually and methodologically flawed position.

In this way such an analysis of child-rearing practices and the formulation of individualism as an ideology leave many questions unanswered. It does not explain, for example, how people can exhibit markedly different traits when they are said to be the product of a relatively homogenous upbringing. Scheman also falls into the trap of criticizing liberalism with its own internal terms, hence reducing the strength of her position. For instance, Scheman defines ideology as a form of altered consciousness, of which individualism and patriarchy are products. This is the liberal definition of ideology formulated within the structures of an empiricist philosophy of science. Ideology is defined in opposition to science which will represent true reality; in this way ideology becomes the simple misapprehension of a certain reality. Scheman needs to give an account of the mechanism by which one would arrive at true consciousness, or otherwise her analysis could simply be another form of deception which, by her criteria, is an important failing. Scheman is appealing to the same universal idea of truth embedded in the Modernist tradition that she criticizes. She needs to provide an explanation of why her feminist interpretation is not just another example of distorted consciousness, unless it is to fall into the abyss of ideological subjectivity.

Nevertheless, while there are problems with Scheman's analysis, her work still makes a valuable contribution to the debate. Scheman's recognition that an individualism of method cannot be separated from an individualism of substance is an important development and one that has interesting practical-political ramifications.

However, Scheman's critique fails to strike at the heart of the problem; the conception of society and the individual as two opposing polarities is still not overcome in her analysis. She formulates the answer to the problem of individualism in terms of shifting the locus of causation on to society, and even with an improved theory of human nature, setting the problem up in these terms will always lead to conceptual difficulties. It is attempting to refute individualism by using its own criteria and mechanisms; what is needed is a restructuring of the very framework in which the debate operates.

## Conclusion

It can be seen that the traditional debate between the individualists and the holists reaches stalemate because it rests on incompatible philosophical positions based on inherent assumption about human nature. The way forward is not by trying to prise away these conceptions of the subject from the doctrines that surround individualism (such as liberalism) because these doctrines themselves are inextricably based on this very formulation of what it is to be human. This conception of human nature provides a certain objective grounding for the presuppositions of liberal theory, without which its very claims to validity and universal application would fall. Take away these theories of human nature and the whole edifice of classical liberalism would collapse. Scheman's theorizing goes some way to overcoming these difficulties but still retains a liberal conception of ideology and a firm commitment to the individual-society dichotomy. It is not an adequate answer to simply shift the locus of causation on to the side of society, as this simply reiterates the same problems. This issue will be expanded and developed in the following chapter.

# Notes

1.  For a collection of essays exemplifying this deadlock, see. O'Neill,J. (1973), (ed.), *Modes of Individualism & Collectivism,* Heinmann, London.

2.  See: Cooley,C.H. (1912), *Human Nature and the Social Order,* New York. Ginsberg,M. (1956), "The Individual and Society", in *On the Diversity of Morals,* London. These are examples of authors trying to resolve the debate within such a framework.

3.  For a critique of reductionism, see. Rose,S et al. (1985), *Not in Our Genes,* Penguin, London.

4.  See Mandelbaum,M. (1973), "Societal Facts", in O'Neill.

5.  For a further exposition of individualism see. Lukes,S. (1985), *Individualism,* Basil Blackwell, Oxford. Hayek,F.A. (1952), *The Counter Revolution of Science,* Glencoe, Ill. Popper,K.R. (1977), *The Open Society & its Enemies,* Vol.1&2, Routledge & Kegan Paul, London. Popper. (1979), *The Poverty of Historicism,* Routledge & Kegan Paul, London. Hayek. (1949), *Individualism & the Economic Order,* London. Ryan,A. (1984), *The Philosophy of the Social Sciences,* Macmillan, London.

6.  For opponents of individualism see the essays in O'Neill.

7.  See James,S. (1984), *The Content of Social Explanation,* Cambridge University Press, Cambridge. James sums up her position on reductionism: "The claim is asserted with more fervour than is justified, since the case for reduction is by no means watertight. In the first place it is founded on a number of assumptions that many holists would reject. And equally important it is made at a level of generality which has little connection with the work of social scientists." (1984:55)

8.  See: (Hayek,1987)

9.  This is a position similar to Hayek's.

10. This can be exemplified by the way women have been perceived as different to men in Western thought. See, Briody Mahowald,M. (1978), *Philosophy of Women: Classical to Current Concepts,* Hackett Publishing, Indianapolis.

11. See Grimshaw (1986), for an elaboration of this point. Also see, Lamb,D. (1979), *Language and Perception in Hegel and Wittingstein,* Avebury, Amersham.

12. See Feinberg,J. (1973), *Social Philosophy*, Prentice-Hall, New Jersey.

13. See Scidentop,L. (1979), "Two Liberal Traditions", in Ryan,A. (ed.), *The Idea of Freedom: Essays in Honour of Isaiah Berlin,* Oxford University Press, Oxford.

14. For a further elaboration of the relationship between liberalism and a concept of society see, Jagger,A. (1983), *Feminist Politics & Human Nature,* Harvester, Sussex. She raises the point:

> Just as the egoistic conception of rationality is inadequate for economics, it is inappropriate for political theory. A number of philosophers have argued that the degree of individual want satisfaction cannot be the criterion for measuring the good society. R.P.Wolff has attempted to summarize many of these arguments by claiming that a political philosophy founded on the value of individual want satisfaction can never admit what he calls the values of community. The egoistic model of human nature is unable to acknowledge the values intrinsic to participating in an affective, a productive or rational community because these values involve, by definition, a concern for individuals other than oneself. Wolff suggests that the values of community constitute legitimate parts of a conception of the public good that cannot be reduced to the sum of individuals' private goods. A theoretical model that does not allow us even to formulate the question whether or not these values should be part of our conception of the public good must be considered seriously inadequate. (1983:45)

# 2 Problems created by the individual–society dichotomy

## Introduction

In the previous chapter it was argued that individualism is based on an implicit theory of human nature. The present chapter extends this analysis and concentrates on the effects this theory has for social explanation. The individualistic notion of an abstract, unitary subject leads to the postulation of a fundamental dichotomy, a dichotomy between the individual and society. This individual-society dichotomy will be examined, arguing that attempts to theorize the social formulation of the subject encounter conceptual difficulties due to their implicit retention of separate notions of the individual and society. This is illustrated by examining techniques in social and developmental psychology which have attempted to theorize the social constituents of the subject, paying particular attention to the difficulties these projects encounter due to their conception of the individual and society as separate entities. Subsequently, the work of Althusser will be discussed, a theorist who endeavoured to posit the individual as a socially constructed entity and was unable to commensurate the individual and society due to two conceptual errors; an inadequate reformulation of the centrality of the subject and an exclusive reliance on the methodology of an empiricist science.

## The Individual-Society Dichotomy Reconsidered

The debate between the individualists and the holists has been beset by conceptual problems. It has developed into an argument over personal ideologies couched in objective philosophical terms, instead of the neutral discussion both parties feel to be the proper medium for debates of this nature. The essential point, that is often overlooked by the two parties, is the use to which these formulations of causation are put;

they both recognize this but leave it on one side so the debate can be seen to continue in philosophically neutral terms. However, the abstract debate has practical political consequences; if society is regarded as the nexus of causation, then a different form of social organization is required from the one an individualist would infer from his theorizing. Both Popper and Hayek [1] recognize and make much out of this point. Hayek argues that a belief in holistic doctrines would lead inevitably to the primacy of a controlling and manipulative elite and could constitute an intrinsic attack on the personal freedom so safely guarded by the individualistic notions of classical liberalism. When Popper criticizes holism he puts it firmly in this context, attacking both its method and implications, as he states:

> Yet holists not only plan to study the whole of society by an impossible method, they also plan to control and reconstruct our society "as a whole". They prophesy that "the power of the State is bound to increase until the State becomes nearly identical with society". The intuition expressed by this passage is clear enough. It is the totalitarian intuition. The term "society" embraces, of course, all social relations....It is for many reasons quite impossible to control all, or "nearly" all, of these relationships; if only because with every new control of social relationships we create a host of new social relations to be controlled. (Popper,1969:79-80)

On this account Popper makes a clear connection between studying society as a whole and a totalitarian political system: the former would bring totalitarianism one step nearer to realization.

The issue of the scope of social explanation becomes confused when the practical outcome of theories are neglected, or swept under the carpet, in favour of justifying positions in terms of their logical superiority or objectivity - as indeed Popper does when he attempts a refutation of historicism: "I have shown that, for strictly logical reasons, it is impossible for us to predict the future course of history." (Popper,1969:v) The practical results of a theory should be of central importance when it is evaluated. This must be recognized or the grounds of the discussion can be changed without the separate issues receiving adequate clarification. Popper, for example, argues simultaneously that holism is both logically and practically inadequate, leaving one to infer that the logical problems holism encounters are given to shore up Popper's political critique of holism. The critique is based on the repugnance Popper feels for the practical outcome that might result from holding a doctrine of holism, namely, a totalitarian and centralized state.

Thus, although such theorists are aware of the practical implications of their theorizing, it is an implicit recognition and one that is seen as peripheral to the discussion once the conceptual perimeters of the debate have been established, concentrating on the logical and metaphysical repercussions. This leaves philosophers with a dilemma; on the one hand, they wish only to engage with the conceptual problems created by individualism and holism and the structure of the debate would require this. Whereas on the other hand, a concern with the practical/political implications is keenly felt. However, the structure of the debate allows no outlet for this dimension, it has to be tacked on as an afterthought, due to its conceptual irrelevance.

A concentration on the logical status of holism and individualism can sometimes have the further effect of enabling the neglect of certain implicit assumptions that both doctrines incorporate. In this way a failure to recognize that all these doctrines are built on specific theories of human nature could be a result of the concentration on the ontological and epistemological status of the two doctrines. This could lead to the discussion skirting around the central issues and never hitting upon the fundamental differences between the individualists and the holists and weakening the conceptual rigour of the debate.

The two positions are deemed to be incommensurable and any attempt at synthesis is made impossible under the current formulation, because they are based on conflicting epistemological and ontological premises. Under this construction one is faced with a choice of two polarities and it is not a solution to opt for one or the other, for neither provides an adequate explanation of the complexities of human organization. In this chapter the problems created by simply taking a holistic analysis will also be highlighted, showing that to put the discussion on a level that necessitates the choosing of one polarity over another is an inadequate method of inquiry.

In the previous chapter the debate surrounding the validity of the doctrine of methodological individualism was evaluated. The debate was held to be incapable of resolution because the problem had been seen as one of scope and placement of causation, rather than as a problem of underlying theories of human nature. Consequently, the pertinent questions asked were: "to which side of the individual-society divide should the essential nexus of causation be located?" and "what is the correct and most profitable area for study if we want to fully understand how human beings function?" It was contended that individualism is built on an implicit conception of human nature, namely an abstract individual, while collectivism took for its subject matter a different conception of the individual: an environmentally conditioned subject. In this chapter the idea of setting the debate in these restricting polarities will be considered in further depth. The very formulation of the debate in terms of an individual-society dualism is an inherent problem from the very outset, neither position providing a correct analysis of social causation.

Critics of individualism have rightly argued that to focus exclusively on the individual as the sole area for study limits the analysis to the point where the explanatory power of the theory becomes negligible. To deny society or reduce its importance to the fringes of explanation leads to a one-dimensional and uninformative conceptual schema. The work of many anthropologists has led to a widespread acceptance of the premise that the surroundings in which one grows up will have an effect on subsequent behaviour, traits and opinions and due to such findings the influence of society can no longer be ignored. In order to redress this imbalance between the weight given to individualist explanations and those couched in terms of socially constructed phenomena, attempts have been made to try and relocate the area of study on to the level of society. This sets out to eliminate explanations that derive their basis from a study of the individual and therefore, implicitly, the theories of human nature that individualism incorporates. In this way people's conditioning and historical placement can be brought into the sphere of determining factors, the conceptual range is widened and consequently, the analysis can be inclusive of certain hitherto unconsidered areas.

This is essentially what certain feminist critiques of individualism (see Chapter One) have set out as their conceptual aim: to enlarge the scope of analysis to include societally grounded factors. This begins from the premise that human characteristics are not innately determined, therefore the difference in social positions allocated to the two sexes must be a result of a society that attributes differing roles and status to women on the grounds that they are in some way inferior. Such grounds build on presuppositions that reduce behaviour to biologically determined factors, a thesis which incorporates both reductionist and individualist assumptions.[2]

In order to overcome the presupposition that women are naturally inferior, that they have some innate biological destiny, a contingent cause for oppression has to be found, as opposed to a necessary cause (such as biology) that would remain unchangeable no matter what action was undertaken. Certain feminists and marxist theorists [3] have taken society to be the contingent and hence changeable area, in which the diversity of humanity is produced. Therefore, dominant conceptions of various groups can be challenged and this position enables society to be seen as something flexible and changing rather than a static force that is the embodiment of destiny.

To look at society, instead of the individual utterances of case studies, is a step forward and one that is capable of revealing a much more interesting and diverse analysis of what influences and determines behaviour. Unfortunately, it is not enough simply to shift the locus of analysis on to society and hope to solve all the problems created by individualism with such a relocation. The problems that individualism creates for social theory are two-fold; the first difficulty is the convention that the subject occupies the central position in the theorization. Re-examining the area with which social inquiry should concern itself has to go hand in hand with a re-evaluation of the central position of the subject. If this is not accomplished then this repositioning of causation (on to the side of society) will never be enough either to defeat the claims of rival theories or provide an adequate system that will supersede them. Implicit in this relocation of analysis is the central nature of the subject. Although the terms of the debate have been changed and a whole field of new enquiry opened up, the fundamental idea of the centrality of the subject has been carried forward with the shifting emphasis.

The second problem that individualism bequeaths to the debate over social explanation is the inherent theories of human nature upon which it is based. Hence, the dispute between individualism and collectivism can never be resolved, because the two positions are based on different conceptions of human nature. These implicit assumptions are never brought into the debate and consequently the two positions become conceptually incommensurable. Individualism's inherent theory of human nature is a coherent doctrine, the abstract, unitary, rational being, and this provides individualism with a solid conceptual base. Whereas collectivism does not have such a solid basis on which to build its schema. Collectivism attempts to manufacture an environmentally determined subject, but is not able to adequately formulate this social construction. The problems with this social construction of the subject are a result of collectivism incorporating two tenets from abstract individualism. First, a notion of a pre-given, unitary subject - that at some point in its development becomes a social being with the juncture at which this happens never being clearly articulated. The second tenet is the central positioning of the subject in analysis. Thus, although collectivism advocates an alternative construction of the subject to the one put forward by individualism, this alternative is merely tacking on social influence to individualism's pre-given subjectivity. In this way collectivism has, in effect, weakened its case by taking these formulations of the subject into its analysis. Neither one of the social theories will ever be able to gain precedent over the other, as the battle is fought over subsidiary arguments, for example the ontological status of societal facts, and the debate is often couched in terms that only one set of theorists would agree upon and hence is incapable of resolution.

Collectivists have challenged the doctrine of individualism and have attempted to supersede it by focussing solely on societal concepts. However, to concentrate solely on society leads to problems similar to those which individualism encounters; those of negating an essential part of human experience. Consequently, this creates an indefensible position. Because society is made up of many individuals and is seen as an amalgam of their wants, aims and behaviour, the collectivist will always be open to the charge that since the individual patently exists it should occupy a central place in theorizing, while society is a concept built upon these existing entities and therefore should not be the definitive area for study. It is more difficult to define what constitutes society than what constitutes an individual and, in the current formulation of the debate, this is a problematic argument for any collectivist position.

In this way collectivism places the subject at the centre of social theory and this leads to a theoretical weakness: the subject is still the primary object of study. Even under the collectivist analysis the subject is constructed as a pre-given entity in the same way as the individualists conceive it. Both theories begin with this pre-given entity, the individual, the person, the object of study, only diverging at the point when this subject enters society or interacts with others. For individualism it is essentially the notion of the abstract individual that characterizes this process; the subject is an unchanging entity and is not capable of radical alteration by its social context in any significant way. Hence society's arrangements are the natural result of human nature.

For collectivism the process is more interesting but nevertheless runs along similar lines. This pre-given subject will be moulded and influenced by the social environment in which it finds itself. Different societies will produce different types of individuals and it is society that, in the final analysis, will determine exactly what a person will be like and how they will see themselves. Unfortunately, collectivism does not adequately formulate this relationship between the individual and the environment. This analysis still incorporates the pre-given subject and it is this notion that has to be problematized from the outset, as it leads inevitably to the subject occupying the central place in social theory however it is subsequently constituted. This applies whether it is a socially produced subject or a biologically (innately) programmed one.

To summarize, the individualistic legacy in social theory operates on two levels: first, the notion of the abstract pre-given subject and second, the central positioning of this subject. The first premise necessitates the second, as it forms the subject into a discrete and unchanging unit, which results in the ability to regard the subject as the correct area for study and concentration. The central place of the subject manifests itself in the predominant methodology of all social theories, so they become theories that concern themselves primarily with the aims, motives and behaviours of individuals however constituted, rather than looking at institutions or other such entities which might, for instance, influence the categories in which we place the subject. The subject of study does not always have to be coterminous with the individual, but social theory conventionally sees its subject as such. [4]

The central place of the subject builds on an abstract, individualist formulation of what it is to be human. It is important to recognize that it is this first presupposition about the character of subjectivity that leads to the placement of the subject at the centre of analysis and allows the dualism between the individual and society to be perpetuated, perpetuated because collectivism cannot formulate the social construction of the subject adequately if this formulation of the subject is retained. It is this idea of a pre-given subject (the individual), even if it is fundamentally influenced by external factors (society), which needs to be challenged. An adequate analysis of how the subject is socially constituted is fraught with tensions if this pre-given subject is retained and prevents the resolution of the individual-society dichotomy. In this way, the collectivist construction of subjectivity is only superficially distinct from that of individualism, the retention of the pre-given subject enables individualism to have more far-reaching effects on social theory than has traditionally been supposed. These points are illustrated by looking at the attempts of social psychology to give socially conditioned factors a place in an individual's development.

## Psychology and Social Construction

The dichotomy between the individual and society is most clearly illustrated within the discipline of psychology, because this is an area that is explicitly concerned with what constitutes human beings and what affects their behaviour, motivations and wants. It is also an area which has based its theorizing on many implicitly held philosophical premises - implicitly held because they are assumptions that have never been open to discussion in the context of mainstream psychology. Although areas such as social psychology have gone some way to challenging these dominant mechanisms of conceptualizing people, [5] fundamentally, psychology still puts the validation for its results firmly on an adherence to alleged scientific rigour and research methods. This results, once psychology had become sufficiently scientific in its outlook and methodology to make such a project feasible, in its goal being one of making behaviour capable of explanation in purely mechanistic and physiological terms. The dangers of doing otherwise are forcefully articulated by D E Broadbent:

> Let me return to my beginning, and say I do not think these questions can be answered without experiment and observation on actual human performance. I promised earlier to take up the question of moral quality of such experiments, and said I thought it would be preferable to use an empiricist method than any of its alternatives. We can tell nothing of our fellow man except by seeing what they do or say in particular circumstances. If one dispenses with this procedure, and so claim to be treating other people as persons rather than machines, one is exposed to the danger of assuming that everyone should be the kind of person one is oneself. In the best of human reasoning and imagination, there is a region of uncertainty because of difficulties of definition, of emotional bias or of habits of thought: and in the physical science the explosive rise of the experimental method in the seventeenth century was a reaction against the savage inhumanity which has burst upon the world as a result of dogmatic theorizing. (Broadbent,1973:206)

And in the words of C L Hull:

> Progress in this area will consist in the laborious writing down, one by one, of hundreds of equations; in the experimental determination, one by one, of hundreds of empirical constraints contained in the equation, etc etc. (Hull,1943:400)

46

These exerpts articulate the view that behaviour can be reduced to automatic and mechanistic processes and therefore become subject to regimentation and objectification. Hence, psychology can elevate its status within academia by employing these methods of scientific quantification. [6]

The idea that behaviour is ultimately reducible to machine-like functionings has obvious implications for attempts to provide a theory of behaviour in a social context - it renders these attempts meaningless. Not only does this view, to a large extent, preclude a notion of societal influence in any aspect, it also theorizes the determination of behaviour in such a way that it solely resides in the physiological functioning of the human brain. Outside factors become relegated to secondary importance because they do not determine behaviour in the final instance, and most importantly, they are not amenable to scientific measurement. Therefore, social influences have to remain in the realm of uncertainty and opinion (not the correct field of study for a scientific psychologist).

The physiological explanation of human behaviour also gives full support to the notion of a pre-given, inherently constituted subject. In this analysis no room is left for change by external factors, it would be impossible to conceive of these factors affecting the brain patterns of an individual, the area where such theorists concentrate their research impetus. [7] The individual is conceived as having certain brain patterns and states motivated by chemicals which can be triggered off, thus producing behavioural patterns. The social environment of the individual is of secondary importance in this process because it can only trigger, not create, these functionings of the brain. The social contribution to behavioural development under this analysis should not be considered, as it is not believed to be capable of scientific investigation (methodologically inadequate) and is not the area where ultimate explanation lies (conceptually inadequate). To illustrate these points and clarify the argument, the way that these issues are dealt with by the practical discipline of social psychology will be considered.

## Psychology's Treatment of Social Formation

It is against this background that social and developmental psychologists have started to rethink the links between biology and society, trying to give an adequate account of the social formulation of individuals. It is in the difficulty such theorists have in conceptualizing the links between an individual and its social situation that the tensions mentioned earlier are saliently highlighted. The difficulties arise in the attempt to rework such a relationship, because the essential dichotomy is left untouched; they perceive the individual and society as two separate entities existing on dissimilar ontological levels. The distinction drawn in this way makes interaction between the two concepts problematic. The debate is still framed in terms of two opposing categories and amalgamation is unlikely to succeed within the discipline of social psychology if it simply rejects the experimental psychologists' methodology while still retaining their conceptual framework. This theorization of social influence has been the concern of social and developmental psychologists and the work of two theorists, M Richards and J Shotter, will be considered as exemplifying this concern.

The developmental psychologist Richards considers what affects a child's development and it is here that the influence society has on an individual is a pertinent question. These issues are addressed in a collection of essays edited by Richards, (1974) that set out to try and formulate the effects society can have on children. This collection breaks new ground by arguing for the need to increase the links between developmental psychology and other less conventionally scientific disciplines (such as sociology) and by attempting to bridge the individual-society divide. The conceptual framework of the debate is determined by the central question posed in the collection - one of how society socializes the individual. This is a laudable aim but Richards prejudices his project by continuing to work within restricting conceptual parameters, failing to examine the area of how the individual is constituted in the first instance. Richards does not explain why he takes a causational process, (one running from the individual to society), as the definitive area for study. To formulate the terminology of the debate in this way results in the inability to resolve the dichotomy because the individual and society are conceived as ontologically opposed entities from the outset. As Richards says in the introduction to the collection, "it is concerned with the process by which an infant becomes a competent member of his social community and develops the fundamental human attributes of speech, social communication, thought, self-reflection and consciousness." (1974:1)

Accordingly, the relationship between the individual and society becomes one of interaction, with the societal influences building on the already existing individual. This interaction is conceived in a minimal sense, which is necessitated by their formulation as two distinct entities. The individual and society can also pull in opposite directions, since they are essentially formulated as antithetical. Society can be influenced by the individual, for example, because it is made up of such individuals, but the individual is not influenced by society in the same way. This builds on the ontological assumption that parts are prior to wholes and results from the posing of the question in such a form.

Due to this conceptual legacy, the project becomes one of trying to gauge how and at what point in its development an infant becomes a social being. The infant, as Richards states, "is not fully social as he is not yet a competent member of a social community", but, "a biological organism with biological propensities and organisation who becomes social through his encounters with social adults. So throughout development there is an essential tension between the biological and the social." (1974:1) In this way the dichotomy remains an intact and problematic concept.

The debate over how society socializes the individual is formulated in such a way that it immediately presupposes some kind of biologically determined, pre-given subject that becomes socialized at a certain point in its development. This retains the dichotomy, as the notion of an abstract individual is still inherent in the theory, leaving an area where the individual and society will be incommensurable. Setting the question in these terms makes the construction of societal influence a very hard and complex project. Given this pre-given subject to build upon, the social has to interact with something that is pre-existent. This raises a complex logical problem which is created by seeing the nature of social influence as something that acts upon a pre-given subject. It is necessary to determine the nature of this entity, which must already exist in some prior form in order that it can be affected by society's persuasion. In the words of Henriques: "It is the age-old problem of the homunculus again: the prior entity which rears its head (sacred or profane depending on the epoch)." (Henriques et al.,1984:97)

To begin the project of giving the "social" a place in the causation of behaviour by posing the problem in this form is to jeopardize it from the start. This approach proceeds from the implicit assumptions of individualism and biological determinism; that people are innately constituted and social influence is the icing on the cake, not the realm where core traits are formed. This is, in effect, arguing for the social determination of an already existing entity with, presumably, already existing qualities. This inevitably creates conceptual and logical problems, for as long as "individual" and "society" are conceptualized as two separate terms, the arguments for the social construction of the subject will remain weak and problematic.

The work of Shotter (1974 & 1974a) is another widely influential attempt to formulate the place of the social in an individual's development. He criticizes traditional psychology on the grounds that its empiricist/scientific emphasis has had profound implications for our images of man. Under this account an empiricist methodology will necessitate certain presuppositions about human nature, resulting in a static, abstract theory, which conforms to mechanistic structures. A crucial aspect of his work is his placing of psychology within an historical and ideological setting in which he traces the historical background of what we call the subject: the formulation of the rational, unitary, Cartesian individual set apart from the world. (1974a:Chapter 5)

Shotter argues that psychology constitutes an ideological theory and affects our image of man in two ways, viz, explicitly and implicitly. Given a specific formulation of what it is to be a normal, rational person, psychology works within this to discover the behavioural paths and delimitations: "Explicitly, we can think of modern psychology as working on what I would like to call image realization; that is, given a particular image of man's nature, it works to discover, or to realize in behaviour, the possibilities inherent in it." (1974a:26) In this formulation of the image of man, psychology sets itself out simply to articulate what is there before it, providing a descriptive function, simply making sense of already existing behavioural patterns. This function of psychology is the traditional role it defines for itself, namely, psychology operates to describe, categorize and treat existing behaviour, not to influence how this behaviour is conceived.

However, more importantly, psychology affects our image of man implicitly by bringing in new notions of human nature rather than just working within existing frameworks. Shotter calls this image replacement: "That is, instead of working to clarify and help in the practical realization of our already "given" but admittedly rather vague image of ourselves as persons, it works to bring in new notions to replace such everyday ideas." (1974a:27) In this way, psychology becomes more than just a mere probing into behavioural patterns, it exerts an influence on what human nature is actually thought to consist of, creating new categories and definitions. This process works implicitly because it is not part of psychology's expressed aim, psychology as a scientific discipline should be merely reporting, not dictating. Shotter points out that this aim is overreached, as psychology also influences and creates images. Psychology then presents these findings as scientifically valid, hence, "implicit acceptance is gained for the underlying hypothesis." (1974a:28) Consequently, psychology implicitly defines and constructs new notions of human nature and gives them the validity of scientific findings, thus these theories of human nature are deemed to be objectively verifiable and usually constructed as innately determined (and hence unchangeable). This is an unjustified methodology by psychology's own criteria, criteria which should reflect the rigours of scientific methodology.

It is because of the implicit influence psychology exerts that makes Shotter profoundly critical of the direction it has pursued, arguing along with S Koch that psychology rests on philosophical foundations long vacated by the philosophers themselves:

> There is a strange circularity, then, in the predicament of psychology. Psychology has long been hamstrung by an inadequate conception of the nature of knowledge, one not of its own making. A world now in motion towards a more adequate conception begins to perceive that only psychology can implement it. Yet psychology is prevented from doing so because, almost alone in the scholarly community, it remains in the grip of the old conception. (Koch,1964:5)

Experimental method and a reliance on the certainty and objectivity of science have been the mainstays of modern psychology. It is this dressing up of emotive and tenuous theories as scientific truths which, argues Shotter, is particularly damaging. The main tenets of this outmoded philosophy are summed up when he discusses cognitive psychology:

The views of an old and outdated philosophy condition its every aspect: [1] the use of experiments to confirm or refute abstract structural models, [2] the talk of mechanisms and the search for their principles of operation, [3] the idea that "we" have no immediate access to reality, and [4] the idea that our knowledge of things is enshrined or encoded as "information". (1974a:58)

Under this account psychology applies to behavioural patterns an empiricist scientific method, a method that Shotter argues is singly inappropriate when related to humans.

In the light of this Shotter attempts to rectify the situation by introducing the role of the social into his work, hoping that this will necessitate a less scientifically orientated methodology and overcome the problem of psychology incorporating a theory of human nature formulated in the Cartesian mould. His alternative system is based on the premise that the development of a child involves some necessary social product such as the interaction of ideologies, class, thought and deliberation. Under this account a child's humanity will be transmitted to it after birth by its interaction with other humans. (Shotter,1974b)

This formulation of the social influences on a child fall into the same conceptual abyss as Richards' question, viz, what is the nature of this entity that becomes a socialized being after certain experiences? The individual-society dichotomy is maintained because Shotter retains the notion of a pre-given subject. The Cartesian subject is not banished so easily, it is not enough to step over the divide and embrace the social. The very central placement of the subject must also be considered and removed from its position of eminence if such an approach is to work. The value of accounts such as Shotter's is the attention they give to the problems incurred by the scientific status of psychology. To see psychology in its subjective and prescriptive role is a first step in the move away from psychology holding the unitary pre-given subject as a definition of what constitutes individuality.

With these examples it is possible to see the difficulties that the notion of social formulation runs into if conceived in this form. There have been many radical critiques of psychology that have set themselves the task of eradicating individualism in psychology, [8] but the approaches seem destined to be perpetually weakened if only the surface problems are dealt with. A fundamental shifting of the centrality of the subject is an essential prerequisite for full-scale change.

## Social Theory and Social Construction

There have been many theoretical positions that have addressed themselves to the issue of the subject's place in social formation and therefore have direct relevance for the consideration of the individual-society dualism. A lucid evaluation of some recent attempts to reconstitute the individualistic notion of the unitary individual at the centre of analysis is provided in *Changing the Subject* by Henriques et al., and, by way of an introduction to the debate, I shall turn to their account. The value of Henriques' account is that it deals explicitly with various effects the individual-society dichotomy can have on social theory. Their analysis illustrates the problems to which a new conception of the placement of the subject needs to address itself and the direction such a study should take. Then the work of Althusser will be examined as a further demonstration of the conceptual problems involved in the theorization of social influence.

In Henriques' analysis the entity that psychology and social theory take as their central subject, namely the rational individual, is identified as the crucial problem for both disciplines. Once this has been established an attempt is made to deconstruct this notion. It becomes immediately apparent that this formulation of the subject is shored up by the philosophical underpinnings of long established social theory and it is to this that they turn: "We approach the deconstruction of the central object of psychology, namely the individual subject, by way of the debate around humanism in Marxism. This will enable us to introduce a number of key concepts which have become the currency of the retheorization of subjectivity." (Henriques,1984:93)

The salient points raised in this debate are those which focus on the place the subject occupies in social change, as opposed to other factors such as economics, class or group action. The humanist position would give the individual a paramount role in constituting all social phenomena and place the individual at the centre of the knowledge-producing process:

> The specific notion of the individual contained in this outlook is one of a unitary, essentially non-contradictory and above all rational entity. It is the Cartesian subject in modern form; a notion of the subject which has been central to the whole of Western Philosophy founded on the principle of the cogito. (Henriques,1984:93)

Humanism rests its case on a defence of human freedom, arguing that a social system that gave precedent to a notion of groups and social wholes would result in the neglect of the individuals that made up these wholes and would validate totalitarianism (a position similar to Popper).

> By and large, then, the humanist position asserted by the left stood for the defence of "human freedom" and pleasures against the oppressive practices of the Soviet Gulags and the implied suppression of the individual in socialist strategies which advocated the subordination of individual needs to the goal of establishing a socialist state. (Henriques,1984:94)

This is an expression of the concern that without adopting a humanistic position that places a value on intrinsic qualities inherent in humanity, there can be no basis from which to defend fundamental human rights. In this way, humanism has sought to protect the individual from coercion by giving it a central status in its epistemological system and conceptual primacy over the idea of society.

The opponents of humanism (some Marxists and Structuralists for example) locate the mechanisms of change firmly on the society side of the dichotomy. It was the central place of the individual as the sole agent of change to which they directed their criticism, running into similar problems to those social psychology encountered when trying to overcome the primacy of the individual in traditional psychology. Such theorists simply shifted the nexus of causation on to the other side of the divide without trying to resolve the polarity itself. Thus, people would become simply the sum of their social construction, as the individual had lost its position as the sole agent of change. Under this analysis it is possible to argue that humanist fears concerning the eradication of a conceptual basis for human rights have been justified, as both social constructionists and postmodernists have been criticized for facilitating the death of man and hence the death of rights that accrue to man. [9] Unless the individual-society dichotomy is resolved the individual is in a precarious position, if causation is located wholly on the society side of the dichotomy.

The problems such an approach encounters are examined in greater detail in the next section. The work of Althusser, a theorist who brought the humanist/anti-humanist debate (that had largely flourished on the continent) to a wider British audience, will be discussed

## Althusser and Social Construction

Althusser's anti-humanist position gives a clear illustration of the conceptual difficulties in such an attempt to give the social a central place in theorizing, and thus his work is considered as an example of the theoretical difficulties brought up by such a project. Althusser attacks the centrality which humanism gives to the subject on the grounds that it is a bourgeois construct to attribute agency solely to the individual. This placing of the individual at the centre of analysis precludes the consideration of such factors as the influence of class and state apparatus on the development of the individual. It is crucial for Althusser to overcome both the pre-given nature of the individual and the central place it occupies in theory in order to argue for the existence of persuasive binding factors by which the state controls its populace. [10]

The subject must be removed from the centre of analysis and replaced by a theory that gives primacy to the social formulation of the individual. In advocating this position Althusser has to find an answer that does not give primacy to either the subject or the structure. To do so would lead to an inadequate solution to the fundamental problem of trying to account for both the role of society in social theory and also the place of the individual. Thus in fulfilment of his task to provide Marxism "with the philosophy" it deserves and repudiate humanism, Althusser had to reject economism in Marxism. An economism which gives sole primacy to the structure and negates the role of other factors such as ideology (which Althusser deemed as essential for capitalism's control of the populace) is not, for Althusser, an adequate basis for a theory. For Marxism to be a viable theory it has to be able to account for a wider range of causes than just those that concern the means of production.

The difficulties in this approach are clear: in rejecting the theory of class reductionism (which sees everything reducible to class positions) another explanation of human conduct has to be postulated which does not simply privilege the structures and which does not reintroduce the humanist formulation of the individual through the back door as the locus of causation.

Althusser's dilemma comes back to the fundamental question: is the subject constitutive or is it constituted? Althusser gives two somewhat contradictory answers to this problem, oscillating between advocating the constitution of the subject by external social factors, and then banishing the subject from theorization when he talks of science as a "theoretical practice" without a subject. In this way the subject becomes a static entity unaffected by outside influences. Althusser postulates science as a subjectless enterprise by severing "theoretical practice" from the "direct discovery of reality". The product of theory is scientific fact, but:

> the process that produces the concrete-knowledge takes place wholly in the theoretical practice: of course, it does concern the concrete-real, but this concrete-real "survives in its independence after as before, outside thought" (Marx), without it ever being possible to confuse it with that other "concrete" which is the knowledge of it. (1969:186)

Hence, science becomes an abstract entity, functioning on a level that has no need for a human subject. Science in this sense is objective and timeless, so the position of the subject in the knowledge-producing process is irrelevant.

Althusser then divides "theoretical practice" into three stages, Generality I, Generality II, and Generality III:

> I shall call Theory (with a capital T), general theory, that is, the Theory of practice in general, itself elaborated on the basis of the Theory of existing theoretical practices (of the sciences) [Generality II], which transforms into "knowledges" (scientific truths) [Generality III] the ideological product of existing "empirical practices" (the concrete activity of men) [Generality I]. (1969:168)

Therefore scientific knowledge [Generality III] will have a different relation to reality than ideology [Generality I]. This throws further light on the idea of science as a body of knowledge that does not need a subject to give it meaning or affect its truth value.

The idea of a "theoretical practice" without a subject is necessary to give historical materialism the scientific status that could protect it from being classed as an ideological theory, that only represents subjective interests. In this theory the individual, as the agent for social change, is replaced by the notion of class struggle, and from this it follows that historical materialism can be advanced as a scientific theory.

This conception of science as a reflection of an unchanging and an ultimately knowable reality is incorporated into Althusser's theory. This leads him into difficulties, which are illustrated when he attempts to make an adequate conceptualization of how, within this empiricist notion of science, the subject is formulated. For Althusser there is a clear distinction to be made between ideology and science: "A science is obtained on condition that the domain in which ideology believes it is dealing with the real is abandoned, that is, by abandoning its ideological problematic...and going on to establish the activity of the new theory "in another element", in the field of a new scientific, problematic." (1969:193) One can separate the area of ideological ideas as a form of distorted knowledge from the correct perception of reality that is provided by science:

> There is no true critique which is not immanent and already real and material before it is conscious....If we carry our analysis of this condition a little further we an easily find in it Marx's fundamental principle that it is impossible for any form of ideological consciousness to contain in itself, through its own internal dialectic, an escape from itself, that, strictly speaking, there is no dialectic of consciousness: no dialectic of consciousness which could reach reality itself by virtue of its own contradictions; in short, there can be no "phenomenology" in the Hegelian sense: for consciousness does not accede to the real through its own internal development, but by the radical discovery of what is other than itself. (1969:143)

It is this reliance on the formulation of knowledge outside the individual consciousness and an appeal to the tenets of science to explain reality, which are often distorted by ideological premises, that leaves the subject in a difficult position within Althusser's theory. Science becomes the true formulation of reality, not contingent on the observers opinions, prejudices, wants, aims or presuppositions. Science conceived in this way has to be built on the ideal of a "rational man". Althusser holds the view that science is a correct exemplar of reality and scientificity is a desirable goal. With this account Althusser formulates a positivist notion of science [11] in which science is the antithesis of ideology and scientific truth the antithesis of ideological error. [12]

Althusser's acceptance of the conventional view of science creates problems for his formulation of the subject. Adherence to a positivist theory of science and the idea of the social constitution of a subject is a contradictory position. If he tacitly embraces this notion of science, he has either to incorporate the scientific idea of "man" as essentially rational, or he has to separate this idea of "man" from scientific theory, leaving a formulation of science that does not depend on the Cartesian version of human nature. Neither project is adequately accomplished as he wishes to replace the subject in "theoretical practice" with the agency of class struggle, neglecting to state how this radically altered driving force would fit into previous scientific structures which are built around the rational, unitary subject. To incorporate a group dynamic in the gap left by the individual would be a project conceptually marred from the offset.

Althusser needs to present the constitution of individuality as an "always-already" social being while at the same time one that is locked in ideological practices. This would explain the social formulation of individuals without reintroducing the Cartesian, rational subject. Althusser attempts to fulfil this task, to adequately conceptualize the individual, by invoking the idea of "interpellation", a process by which the individual is produced by and in ideological processes. These ideological processes have relative autonomy from the means of production and a different status, hence the ideological is the "imaginary". The distortion of reality, "inadequate to the essence of the objects from which abstraction should extract it", (1969:191) is contrasted with the forces of production which are perceived as "real". This harks back to his conception of science. The forces of production under this analysis take on the status of science in opposition to the "imaginary" ideological apparatus. Such ideological apparatus shores up capitalism by means of institutions such as the family, Church, school and, nowadays, the mass media, producing individuals who will exemplify the characteristic that this form of economic organization demands and deems to be natural.

It is in this way that Althusser formulates the relationship between the subject and ideology, by seeing ideological formulation as "imaginary" he formalizes the process by which people's ideas are autonomous from the means of production and provides a notion of the subject that is also independent of class struggle. The "imaginary" is not made present to the subject by direct perception, it is rather:

> the result of a complex process of elaboration which involves several distinct concrete practices on different levels, empirical, technical and ideological. [Thus] the concept of fruit is itself the product of distinct practices, dietary, agriculture or even magical, religious and ideological practices in its origin. (1969:191)

Ideological state apparatuses influence the subject by a mechanism of "interpellating" subjects. As Henriques states:

> The subject recognises her/himself as such through a process of recognition whereby the authority of the institution and its representatives, for example the parents and teachers, "hail" the

individual. S/he recognises her/himself through this relation, which is imaginary. In this view, the subject does not exist prior to its hailing or interpellation. (Henriques,1984:97)

Consequently, Althusser reintroduces the logical problem mentioned earlier: what is the nature of the entity that must already exist in some prior form in order to recognize itself in this construction of interpellation?

It is his formulation of the "real" world versus the "imaginary" world of ideologies and distorted conceptions that ultimately leads Althusser to an inadequate theory of the processes by which the subject is constituted. The "real" world of the means of production takes on a different status from the "imaginary", and its effects on the subject remain unclarified. He postulates how the "imaginary" permeates the subject so that, by believing and acting as if the "ideologies" were real, people make them the reality in which they live. These ideologies are, by definition, distortions and myths to seduce the populace. The subject will therefore be constituted by the "imaginary" ideological constructs. If people's perception of real and imaginary are the same then this analysis fails to differentiate between the two - how does the "real" affect people in a different way from the "imaginary"?

It is here that the relationship between knowledge and the "real" needs elucidation. [13] Althusser encounters a problem in explaining how these "theoretical practices" relate to reality and indeed each other:

> That the concrete-in-thought [Generality III] under consideration is the knowledge of its object (the concrete-real) is only a "difficulty" for the ideology which transforms this reality into a so-called "problem" (the problem of Knowledge), and which therefore thinks as problematic what has been produced as a non-problematic solution to a real problem by scientific practice itself; the non-problematicity of the relation between an object and the knowledge of it. (1969:186)

In this way Althusser makes a category leap that is neither articulated nor justified, side-stepping the epistemological problem rather than solving it. This problem is one of the relationship between consciousness and the "real". Althusser states that a consciousness cannot accede to the "real" through its own internal development, it does so by a discovery of something other than itself. Such a discovery involves the consciousness in making a leap from thought and speculation to true reality, a leap possible only if the conception of reality held conforms to Platonic idealism. The difficulties this leaves for the social construction of the subject are obvious. Althusser never conclusively overcomes the problem of the homunculus and thus incorporates a notion of the pre-given subject into his analysis. Further, his reliance on an empiricist scientific methodology creates tensions in his treatment of the real versus the imaginary and how such factors could influence the subject. Althusser erects a framework of "interpellation" that needs a conventional scientific methodology to validate its mechanisms.

## Conclusion

It is possible to see how the project of bringing the social into theorization is fraught with tensions no matter how the interaction is formulated if the two terms, individual and society, are kept as conceptually distinct notions. Although strict comparisons between the theories of Althusser and social psychology are not possible, it is clear that they both founder, if they use an empiricist theory of science, to retheorize the place of the subject. To incorporate a notion of social constitution and group dynamics into the structures of conventional science is a daunting task and it is arguable whether it can be achieved. The two positions never overcome the barrier created by conceiving human nature in an abstract individualist framework and the central place the subject occupies in social theory. The subject needs to be relocated, as just one area of study among many, giving priority not to the structure or the subject but reaching an analysis that rests on a synthesis of all causes. In the next chapter the historical construction of the subject in its present form will be examined, illustrating how it has been integral to an empiricist and positivist science. Further, the implications of this subject for the formulation of concepts such as normality, madness and error will be considered.

# Notes

1.    See: Popper,K.R. (1977), *The Open Society and its Enemies,* Routledge & Kegan, London. Hayek,F.A. (1949), *Individualism and the Economic Order,* London. Also see: Popper,K.R. (1965), "Social Science & Social Policy", in Braybrooke,D (ed.), *Philosophical Problems of the Social Sciences,* Macmillan, New York. In which Popper advocates a "piecemeal" approach to social engineering as opposed to a holistic approach. In his view the holistic approach has two flaws: first it is incompatible with a scientific attitude and second, it states that total reconstruction of society is needed and is therefore unable to attack problems with an open mind for the holist has already decided that this total reconstruction must take place without considering the practical expediencies. It is prejudiced from the outset to privilege certain solutions.

2.    For an outline of this position see: Wilson, E.O. (1975), *Sociobiology: The New Synthesis,* Belnap, Cambridge, Mass. Barash,D.P. (1977), *Sociobiology and Behaviour,* Elsevier, New York. For a critique of biological determinism see: Frith, L.J. (1992), "Sociobiology, Ethics and Human Nature" in Lamb,D. (ed.), *New Horizons in the Philosophy of Science,* Avebury, Aldershot.

3.    See: for an account of Marx's philosophy of action, Plamenatz,J. (1975), *Karl Marx's Philosophy of Man,* Oxford University Press, Oxford. & Ollman,B. (1971), *Alienation: Marx's conception of man in capitalist society,* Cambridge University Press, Cambridge. Seve,L. (1978), *Man in Marxist Theory and the Psychology of Personality,* Harvester, Brighton.
      There has been much feminist writing on the issue of human nature and a useful summary of this feminist political thought is, Jagger,A. (1983), *Feminist Politics and Human Nature,* Harvester, Brighton. Lloyd,G. (1984), *The Man of Reason: Male & Female in Western Philosophy,* Methuen, London. This work provides an interesting analysis of the portrayal of women in philosophy. Flax,J. (1983), "Political Philosophy and the Patriarchal Unconscious: A psychoanalytic perspective on epistemology and metaphysics", in Harding & Hintikka (ed.), *Discovering Reality,* D.Reidel Publishing Company, London. Spender,D. (1980), *Man-Made Language,* Routledge & Kegan Paul, London. Spender.(1982), *Women of Ideas (and what men have done to them),* Routledge & Kegan Paul, London. Mitchell,J. (1975), *Psychoanalysis & Feminism,* Vintage Books, New York. Rubin,G. (1975), "The Traffic in Women: Notes on the "Political Economy" of Sex", in Reiter,R, (ed.), *Toward an Anthropology of Women,* Monthly Review Press, New York.

4.    A critique of this position has been long standing from marxism's structuralist social theory to Levi-Strauss's "death of man".

5.    See: Shotter,J. (1975), *Images of man in Psychological Research*, Methuen, London. Harre,R. Clarke,D.   DeCarlo.N. (1985), *Motives and Mechanisms*, Methuen, London.

6.    For a fuller critique of the counter-arguments and arguments for scientism in psychology see: Armistead,N. (1974), (ed.), *Reconstructing Social Psychology*, Penguin, Harmondsworth. Margolis,J. (1984), *Philosophy of Psychology*, Prentice Hall, Englewood Cliffs, NJ. Ingleby,D. (1970), "Ideology and the human sciences", *Human Context,* 2. Harre,R. & Secord,P,F. (1972), *The Explanation of Social Behaviour,* Blackwell, Oxford. Harre et al., (1985) *Motives & Mechanisms.*

7.    Space does not allow this issue to be gone into fully. An example of such a mechanistic explanation of behaviour is the experiment outlined in   Back,K.W. (1977), (ed.)*, Social Psychology,* John Wiley & Sons Inc, Chichester.  In order to account for the crimes committed by the Nazis,  the  argument that the rank and file were simply acting on orders and are not to blame has often been advanced.  To test this hypothesis an experiment was conducted by Stanley Milgram in 1960, an experiment that was designed to evaluate how obediently people followed those in authority. Subjects were  told  to administer what they thought were painful electric shocks to other participants: 26 out of the  40  subjects delivered the most powerful shock simply because they had been told to do so by the instructor. This experiment is advanced as a scientific analysis and applicable to a situation like Nazi Germany. The apparent difficulty in applying this to a social situation and deriving any  meaning  from the findings are never dealt with by the experimental psychologist and it is unproblematically assumed that the laboratory experiment is directly analogous to a complex socio-political situation.

8.    See Harre, et al., *Motives and Mechanisms,* op cit., This develops an explicit critique of individualism and tries to set up a new basis for psychology to combat these tensions. However, in the last instance unsuccessfully because it retains the individual-society dichotomy. In their words, there could be,

      the possibility of picking out an entity, a social entity, on which to practice psychological investigations. If the processes of rational decision-making, of remembering, and so on, could be said to occur in social groups as well as in individual persons, the boundary between individual and society would dissolve. Individualism denies such investigations would be appropriate to any such entity, though specific forms of association such as families, groups at work or crowds might seem to exhibit autonomous psychological processes. If it were possible to prove that groups, families or crowds were merely surface phenomena and their process social only in so far as they were surface too, it would follow that the concealed cognitive processes in collectives are actually concealed in individuals, just as they are assumed to be in individual psychology. As such they are not social by nature, although they may be dubbed "social" by virtue of having exclusively social products. Social products need not have social origins. (1985:66)

9.  See the discussion in Chapter Four.

10. For a wider analysis of Althusser's work in a practical context see, Elliott,G. (1988), *Althusser: The Detour of Theory,* Verso, London.

11. See Larrain,J. (1979), *The Concept of Ideology,* Hutchinson and Co Ltd, London. For a discussion of Althusser's philosophy of science based on Bachelard and one that can be characterized as positivism: "It seems to me that Bachelardian philosophy of science which Althusser incorporates into Marxism is in the best tradition of positivism and opposes science to ideology in the same way as the rational opposes the irrational." (1979:197) This is a critique of Althusser's theory of truth, a theory in which he constructs truth as the opposite of error and therefore science as the opposite of ideology and his argument that science is coterminous with truth. Also see: Lichtheim,G. (1967), *The Concept of Ideology and other Essays,* Random House. Plamenatz,J. (1971), *Ideology,* Macmillan, London.

12. See: Althusser,L. (1976), *Essays in Self-Criticism,* (G Lode trans), New Left Books, London.

13. An examination of Althusser's epistemology and methodology is given by Brown in the form of a comparison with Foucault and Derrida, (see Chapter Four for an analysis of Foucault's formulation of the subject). Brown,P.L. (1975), "Epistemology and Method: Althusser, Foucault, Derrida", *Cultural Hermenutics,* Vol 3, No 2.

# 3  The historical formulation of the subject

## Introduction

This chapter will discuss the formulation of the unitary abstract subject in greater depth, attempting to illustrate and develop two points. First, the abstract unitary theory of human nature is a historically specific entity, arising out of certain social circumstances; and, secondly, this construction    is the formulation of  humanity upon which the conceptual schema of psychology  is built. Once this theory of the subject is taken to represent what human nature really is, then it can be  used  as a  controlling tool, operating as a normative, rather than as a purely descriptive, concept. With  this  formulation of the  subject  being regarded as a natural and universal exposition of humanity, it has subsequently been used as a measure against which concepts   such   as sanity and normality can be judged.  Normality has to be  posited against a standard of what humanity is naturally like; hence making  this subject integral  to  concepts  of  error, madness and insanity. These normalizing functions  of  the subject  are  illustrated  by examining social psychology's analysis of racial prejudice and, following abstract theory to  its practical outcome, tracing the implications that this construction of human nature has for the treatment of Afro-Caribbeans by the  psychiatric profession in England. Finally,  the  chapter  will analyse how the discipline of transcultural psychiatry has tried  to  problematize the   discriminating practices  of traditional psychiatry and attempts to provide a different analysis based on the implementation of  culture as a diagnostic tool.

Chapters  One  and  Two  argued that social theories are built on certain implicit assumptions about human nature. It was  contended  that these  assumptions are responsible for the incommensurability of the two dominant  social  theories,  individualism  and  collectivism.  The individualist conception of human nature is one that  characterizes   its subject  as  an abstract and unitary individual.   In this chapter the emergence of this subject will be charted. It is not enough to argue that this conception of the subject exists and point to modern examples of how it functions; the historic specificity of the creation of this subject needs to be examined. Therefore, it is pertinent to ask where this notion of the subject originated and what led to its construction in an abstract and unitary mode. Before going on to analyse this construction of the subject, some aspects of the seventeenth-century revolution in epistemology and scientific thought will be briefly considered to provide an outline of the broader social, economic and political factors that led to the formulation of a new conception of "man". Then the chapter will examine how this conception of the subject has been incorporated into the theoretical framework of psychology as an exposition of what constitutes "natural man" and the implications this has for social psychology's treatment of phenomena such as racial prejudice.

## An Overview of the Changing Cosmology

This account of the change in cosmological formulations will be necessarily brief as it simply seeks to put the historical formulation of the subject into the broader context of general epistemological trends, rather than provide a detailed historical analysis. The account also seeks to place psychology in these wider trends, showing how it too has developed out of a specific historical and social context.

The vast reconstruction of world views that took place around the seventeenth century had a substantial impact on how Western intellectuals (mainly men) conceived and ordered reality. [1] It affected all branches of knowledge, not only the sciences, and challenged the very nature of what was known as "normal man" (or the subject of discourse). This profound change in conceptions of humanity paved the way for the development of what psychology considered to be its basic subject matter: an abstract formulation of human nature. This, and the incorporation of Enlightenment theories into its conceptual framework, modified psychology into the discipline it is today.

The old world view, which comprised a God-centred universe, based on the "great chain of being", perceived human nature to be a static and unchanging amalgam of traits, wants and desires. Humans were put on earth by a God who decreed their characteristics and the hierarchies of social status were similarly ordained from heaven. People were born into their roles and were advised not to try and advance their position beyond their preordained place in the chain, a move that could be construed as going against the will of God, while those who accepted their lot on earth would be rewarded in heaven. This old conception of human nature had to be replaced by a new dynamic, changing subject that could be the driving force behind the developing industrialization of the economy. A conception of humanity that was locked into an unchanging hierarchy would be incongruous with the emerging social system that emphasized advancement (and hence movement up the social scale) by hard work. Further, along with these social considerations, the new rational unitary human being could become an object for scientific enquiry - a role this previously static conception of human nature with God-given characteristics was unable to fulfil. This transdental subject could, with its rational faculties, perceive and order the world into objective categories. When psychology became crystallized into a distinct intellectual discipline it defined itself through this conception of the subject. Psychology modelled itself on natural science and thus became a scientific discipline whose object of study was the mind and the behavioural manifestations that resulted from such a mind.

This rational unitary formulation of the subject that now dominates modern psychology became possible as a result of the foundations set by the mechanistic conception of the world expressed in the work of Descartes, a conception which subsequently became naturalized by the Darwinian theory of evolution. Darwin's theory of natural selection provided the biological underpinnings for this mechanistic theory of human nature. In order to fully understand the emergence of this mechanistic philosophy and evolutionary theory their development must be analysed by examining the social context out of which they arose, viewing these theories both as a response to and a cause of socio-economic forces. As Easlea notes when considering the issue, mechanism did not triumph simply because it explained phenomena more adequately than the old world view:

> The victory of this extraordinary philosophy over its equally extraordinary rival cannot be understood in terms of the relative explanatory successes of each basic cosmology but rather in terms of the fortunes of the social forces identified with each cosmology. (Easlea,1980:91)

Christopher Hill also makes this point - that the new mechanistic philosophy had ramifications for social organization:

> Rejection of non-mechanistic explanations was in part - and only in part - ideologically motivated. Stable laws of nature went with a stable society. Now that God was located within every human heart, it was inconvenient to have him intervening in the day-to-day running of the universe. Both popular magic and Catholic magic upset the ordered cosmos. (Hill,1975:294)

In this way, the various branches of knowledge can be seen to be sharing the same social context out of which they were born, each underwriting the others' claims, each providing a social as well as an epistemological function. Thus, psychology modelled itself on the prevalent epistemologies which had their most formalized articulation in the doctrine of classical physics, incorporating the basic concepts of Newtonian mechanics into its theoretical framework. M Pecheux further elaborates the interwoven and social nature of knowledge formation.

Empiricist as well as realist theories of knowledge, seem to have an interest in forgetting the existence of scientific disciplines as historically constituted, preferring a universal theory of ideas, whether the latter takes the realist forms of a universal and *a priori* network of concepts or the empiricist form of an administrative procedure applicable to the universe conceived as an ensemble of facts, objects, events or acts. (Pecheux,1975:68)

One element in this mechanistic conception of the universe that had deep-rooted and dramatic effects for the formulation of psychology as an autonomous discipline was the mind-body dualism of Descartes. P Manicas states that the bifurcation of mind and matter, and the subsequent relegation of mind to the realm of the metaphysical, was one of the main conceptual developments that formed psychology into the discipline that it is today. Thus, this bifurcation has located psychology's conceptual schema firmly into an essential schism, a schism that is built on the mind-body distinction. The person is now divided into these two elements, mind and body, each requiring different mechanisms of study because they operate on different metaphysical levels.

Descartes defined the parameters of this conceptual framework when he asserted, that: "There is nothing included in the concept of body that belongs to the mind; and nothing in that of mind that belongs to the body." (Sommers,1978:225) Sommers comments on this:

For Descartes the distinction is radical: minds and bodies are of ontologically different types. He compares someone who says that minds are extended to one who says "Bucephalus was music," and he characterizes his own denial that minds are extended to one who is correcting the assertion that Bucephalus is music. If a man asks how much the mind weighs, he needs to be corrected in a radical way, for his question is a category mistake. [Minds] do not have the ontological *features* of extension and thought and the predicates are simply senseless. (1978:225)

Consequently, humanity was understood as consisting of isolated egos existing inside mechanical bodies. Descartes' conception of reality was based on making a fundamental distinction between two realms: that of mind or *res cogitans*, the thinking thing, and that of matter or *res extensa*, the extended thing. For Descartes the mind was to be studied by a process of introspection, while the body should be the object of examination for the natural sciences. This methodology was not strictly adhered to by subsequent generations of psychologists, who elected to divide the mind into external and internal strands and study them separately. This created two major schools: the behaviourists who concentrated on the study of behaviour, resulting in a denial or at least a neglect of the existence of mind; and the structuralists who studied the mind through introspection, analysing consciousness by trying to reduce it to its basic elements. Both schools built on the Cartesian dichotomy, emphasizing the persuasiveness of its influence, each taking its own specific area for study with the possibility of a fusion ruled out by the conceptual framework Descartes bequeathed.

This conceptual framework provided the basis for experimental psychology in the nineteenth century. Figures such as Wundt (1907, 1973) (seen by many as the founder of scientific psychology) drew a clear distinction between mind and matter. In order to know things about the mind it was necessary to use a process of introspection - an analytic method that could allow consciousness to be reduced to well-defined elements associated with specific nerve currents in the brain. With developments in anatomy and physiology during the nineteenth century these reductionist accounts of behaviour flourished producing hypotheses that conformed to such models. This supposition that behaviour could be reduced to a set of independent mental faculties localized in specific regions of the brain and explained by analysing these physiological impulses, is an example of a basic reductionist account of causation and a guiding assumption of experimental psychology. [2] Despite the implausibility of such formulations, the basic aim to associate various emotions and functionings of the mind with precise physical locations in the brain has, in principle, not yet been ultimately rejected and is still flourishing today.

This mind-body split was not the only dichotomy created - the mind itself was also divided into two parts; the physiological and the emotional. On the one hand the mind would be subject, in a similar way to the material world, to laws which would express the quantitative measurement of bodily activities such as motions and regulated associations of ideas. [3] On the other hand, values and emotions would be the domain of the moral sciences, which are essentially subjective disciplines and not sciences in the strict sense. With these developments, psychology could now become a discipline accounting for the errors that the senses induced in the mind by building on this new rational conception of humanity, leaving values and emotions in the hands of the moral philosopher. If man was essentially a rational being then a deviation from what was regarded as the "normal" rational path could be measured against this standard of rationality. Madness, sanity and human error were now elements to be quantified, capable of scientific analysis and objective investigation.

From this, it is possible to envisage how the view of the cosmos changed dramatically from one of a God-centred universe to a cosmos ordered by scientific and rational premises. This changing basis of ultimate causation (moving from God to science), resulted in the creation of a whole new conceptual framework, with science becoming the highest arbiter of truth. Experimental method was the only legitimate form of investigative procedure and elements were to be reduced to their component parts so that they could be understood and analysed properly. All these factors had a dramatic effect on how the individual was perceived and it will be to this that the next section will turn.

## The Historicity of the Subject

The historicity of the subject will now be examined, looking at the account given by C Venn in her article "The Subject of Psychology", which provides an elucidating analysis of the subject's historical formulation. Her article is considered as an example of accounts that attempt to formulate the social construction of individuality and place this in a historical context. She attempts to analyse the effects of mechanistic philosophy and Darwinian evolution on the construction of the subject by employing a Foucaultian methodology seeking, not to give a precise definition of the subject, but to provide a genealogy of its emergence. Venn analyzes the subject by locating it within the many discourses in which it is formed, with this conception of the subject forming other discourses in a similar fashion. The relationship between subject and discourse is reciprocal, where neither holds the final place in causation, but each is interwoven with the other. [4] Venn begins by showing the cultural specificity of the subject by locating it in an historical and epistemological context; the mechanistic discourse needed a rational man to look at this new scientific and rational world. In this way, the abstract individualist formulation of the subject was made possible by and necessitated a positivist science which based itself on a recourse to the rational and needed a rational man who could be the knowing subject in this scientific epistemology.

Venn then looks further into what exactly constitutes this new idea of individuality:

> The subject that I have been describing as the unitary, non-contradictory subject in fact combines a double subjectivity: on the one hand the subject of science and reason born with modern science (and the new social order that replaces feudalism) and on the other, the abstract legal subject, the subject of general rights and of possessive individualism. (1984:133)

The first subjectivity is the unitary rational subject which begins to appear in Western culture from the seventeenth century onwards and becomes the possessor of knowledge. This is a forerunner to an epistemological reductionist view that groups cannot be in possession of knowledge - only individuals can command and create it.

The second subjectivity is the abstract legal subject. This new conception of the individual, in theory, places everyone in an equal position before the law and administration; there should be no *a priori* discrimination. These were the beginnings of the liberal tradition that everyone had a right to equal treatment before the law, regardless of social class, wealth and later gender and race. However, this did not mean that in practice everyone was equally considered. The exclusion of certain members of the community from such an equal standing in relation to the law and the possession of rights was justified on the basis of their supposed inability to make rational decisions. On these grounds Locke was able to exclude the propertyless from proposals for enfranchisement, not because they were "less equal", but because they could not make rational decisions and were therefore incapable of behaving in a responsible and moral fashion. Later Kant located the existence of a rational facility as the crucial element in both the making of moral choices and the grounds on which people were treated as ends in themselves and hence had a claim to be accorded rights and treated fairly.

The universal applicability of the abstract legal subject was kept intact by this method of exclusion. People were only excluded if they could not be described as normal rational persons. Thus, what was defined as rationality became a crucial transection for society and it is this conception of rationality that links the two aspects of the subject's double nature. Further, this conception of rationality was institutionalized and built into the administrative structures. Such an institutionalization enabled the administration to operate on a supposedly objective and rational basis. Once these value judgements achieved universality, they were no longer viewed as anything less than the fair and only way to organize a society.

This formulation of the subject was taken by psychology to be its basic subject matter and Venn attempts to illustrate how the subject of psychology can be seen, not as a value-free objective entity, but as an historically constructed concept. From this it can be argued that the assumptions of psychology, namely that mental processes attach to us singly, are inextricably linked to notions of the individual found in administration and economics. As Venn points out: "Psychology as a science of the social *"interiorizes that connection"*: it produces the identity between the "normal" subject of individualism and that of rationality, and locates that identity inside the subject. Thus it naturalizes that notion of rationality and of normality." (1984:133) In this way, psychology argues that what constructs and defines human nature are solely internal and inherent factors, that are implicit in our biological make up. Psychology then takes this naturalization of reason one stage further and universalizes it, claiming that it is a common characteristic of all humanity. This universal definition of the subject can be studied by the objective scientific disciplines and should also form the bedrock of the liberal tradition of social organisation.

Another factor that further cements the subject into this rationalistic mould is the escalating status given to science, mathematics and logic. These disciplines are now viewed as the most illuminating means of explaining the world, Venn states,

another displacement was also taking place in this long struggle, perhaps more important than the themes I have mentioned: it is

68

the shift which locates Reason and the Subject-of-Reason at the core of that new *ratio*, as its ultimate guarantee. Gradually, rationality and logic come to be regarded as primary: the basic elements of the logocentric subject. (1984:134)

Texts like the scriptures, theology or philosophy are no longer deemed to be capable of revealing the truth as they once were thought to. Science has replaced God as the ultimate location of certainty and truth. [5] The quest for certainty, formulated in the Cartesian manner, has to be located in the realms of science, logic and mathematics. In this way, subjective formulations of the cosmos cannot be trusted, objectivity becomes the only criterion for useful inquiry:

> Thus the birth of the modern subject is tied to the co-articulation of the three themes - Mathesis, mechanism, modern reason and the subject-of-reason - upon which pivots the conceptual framework for an understanding of the world. But there is more than that. For the point is the substitution of "man" for God at the heart of this world, a substitution which makes sense when one considers that man was already God's privileged creation (in *his* image) endowed with reason, and indeed is the only entity or agent who could have filled the place left empty by the evacuation of divine from matter. (1984:136)

Old concepts, such as the "uniqueness of man", were replaced by those of the rational scientific man who took on the functions previously performed by God and religion.

As has been stated, in order that this shift be successfully completed the previous explanation of a divinely created human nature had to be replaced by a more rational and scientific theory. Venn argues that the naturalization of reason in the Darwinian theory of evolution provided the necessary scientific basis for such a theory of human nature. This development made possible the securing of the subject in biology; the subject was now located within a scientific discourse and rationality was shown to be a naturally given trait. An individual's position in society could now be justified in terms of their essential biological nature: "So the human subject is biologized; indeed it has not ceased to find a handy refuge in the soil of biology since that time. Individualism has become the normal because it is now thought to accord to the *natural state* of existence." (1984:145) Darwin began his theorizing by adopting a materialist basis, in direct contradiction to the idea of "the uniqueness of man" which postulated the nature of man as an unchanging entity not amenable to scientific study, bringing humanity within the realms of scientific explanation.

Any theory of evolution must consider how man as a social animal has developed and, as Venn notes, Darwin was not blind to the implications his research had for the explanation of social entities. Under Darwin's schema the formation of commonly held entities, such as language, ethical and asethietic values were to be accounted for in the same terms as those used for physical developments, namely applying the evolutionary selection mechanisms.

This pushed psychology further down the road to becoming a scientific discipline: "Furthermore, the proposition that mind and its capabilities and faculties were amenable to scientific explanations of the same kind as physiological changes clearly brought with it the idea that these capabilities could be investigated using appropriate *scientific* methodologies." (1984:144) Thereafter mind could be viewed as a legitimate object of scientific inquiry, because its formulation was due to the same factors to which physical change was subject. The science of mind could now borrow the characteristic method of the physical sciences - one of experimentation and rigorous quantification.

Venn stresses that this process of the naturalization of reason was one of displacement rather than transformation. The seventeenth-century notion of the individual as a thinking, acting machine does not change, the difference lies in the basis of these characteristics. Previously their origin was held to lie in divine creation, and development was guided by an ultimate spiritual destiny based on religion. With Darwinian theory, nature took over the role of religion, explanations had their basis in the natural process and these processes were amenable to a scientific methodology:

> Henceforth, nature and science mutually underwrite each other's claims. Concerning the mind and the rational processes of the subject, we are referred on the one hand to science in the positivist sense as the measure and the norm, the arbiter of cognition, and, on the other hand, to natural origin and development to account for its present state. (1984:145)

Hence individualism has become the *natural state* of existence, with its ultimate justification found in biology and the subject, so formulated, becomes a representation of natural fact.

The subject now had its place in the scientific framework and this conceptualization has persisted up to the present day. Despite a greater emphasis on the effects society has on an individual's development within the growing field of social psychology, (a discipline which has continually been seen as the poor relation of experimental psychology), the pre-given, unitary nature of the subject is still the prevalent model. The very definitions of social psychology advanced reflect the rigidity and the persuasiveness of psychology's conception of its subject. In a standard text book on social psychology, Otto Khineberg defines the discipline as: "The scientific study of the behaviour of the individual related to other individuals. It is concerned with the individual in a group situation." (Khineberg,1977:2) In the same text Back comments on this and states, "this is a serviceable definition. It describes a boundary around the subject, marks it off from other material, and places a few items in the field thus delineated, such as "individuals" and "groups"." (Ibid)

Khineberg highlights the importance of scientific method in the field of psychology when, in providing a historical overview of the discipline, he states: "Perhaps the most important development in the field of social pscyhology has been the gradual extension of the applicability of experimental, empirical and quantitative methods....These prospects are encouraging for the further development of social psychology as an empirical and objective branch of science." (Khineberg,1960:13-14) These concerns have not changed and social psychology is still defined as, "the scientific study of how people think about, influence and relate to one another." (Myers,1993:3) This method produces a tension between psychology as a scientific and laboratory-orientated discipline and other areas of psychology that try to evaluate the more human concerns of the social sciences. The effects of this construction of human nature on conceptualizations of insanity and deviant behaviour will now be examined.

## Madness and the Conceptualization of Error

This universal rational conception of the subject has acted as a yard-stick against which psychology can measure any deviation from the perceived norm. Once rationality is deemed to be amenable to scientific evaluatation then what is irrational can be quantified similarly and, with the elevation of rationality to the status of *a priori* truth, concepts such as madness and deviation can also become scientifically verifiable. Psychology armed with this scientific methodology is concerned with quantifying and measuring, using deviance as an indicator of the norm. Psychology now concentrates its analysis on examing the manifestations of error - defined as a move away from rational behaviour and preparing extensive studies and experiments in this area.

There have been copious studies of alcoholism, drug addiction, unwanted pregnancies, violence of various sorts and truancy - social situations and personality traits which are deemed to be a deviation from the rational norm. Very few of these studies have been concerned with middle-class life, probably because most of these studies are researched by middle-class academics who do not want to read about themselves and who consider their lifestyle normal. On the other hand, there are many reports and projects on working-class lifestyles, [6] written in a language by and for a different group of people from those under study. To be working class is not directly to be seen as deviant, but it is to be one step removed from the rational ideal with which psychology evaluates people. In this respect, to be less educated is to be less rational and ultimately less normal.

A practical outcome of psychology's concentration on abnormal behaviour is the way in which this definition of abnormality has been used in the process of normalization and disciplining the population. [7] For the structures of administration, deviance presents a problem, for example, in P Pasquino's (1980) study of the police in the eighteenth century, he shows how society became the agency against which crime was defined when a new concept of policing was debated. Classes of people who did not fit into the dominant structures of society or who posed a threat to these structures, such as the unemployed and the propertyless poor during the seventeenth century, were consistently defined as abnormal and dealt with accordingly. Such categories were institutionalized or denied the right to participate in the democratic process, for instance the disenfranchisment of the propertyless poor, who failed to comply with the property qualifications and thus were unable to vote.

An interesting account of the changing perceptions of madness, viewed not simply in an historical framework but from an analytic perspective within the structure of discourse and genealogy, is advanced by M Foucault (1965). Genealogy attempts to retrace the mutual dependencies that exist between social scientific discourses and administrative practices that regulate society's institutions and thus provide an account of the specific conditions of the emergence and production of such discourses. This becomes an investigation into the nature of power as Foucault states:

> I am supposing that in every society the production of discourse is at once controlled, selected, organised and redistributed according to a certain number of procedures, whose role is to avert its power and changes, to cope with chance events, to evade its ponderous, awesome materiality. (Foucault,1971:8)

The issue of the formulation of the subject and the exact construction of power relations are considered in greater detail in the final chapter; here the issues surrounding the latter point, the historicity of the concept of madness, are examined. Foucault considers the history of the transformation of madness, from being regarded as belonging to the bad part of the human soul along with idolatry, luxury, and anger, for instance, to being seen as a highly feared pathology and a source of anxiety, a shift which developed during the sixteenth century. Madness therefore became the weak point in society's new mechanistic framework, where reason could disintegrate into irrationality, a force to be silenced and repressed in order to protect the norms of the rational:

> Madness becomes a form relative to reason, or rather madness and reason enter into a perpetually reversible relation which provides every madness with its reason, that sits in judgement upon and masters it, every reason its madness in which it finds its derisory truth. Each is the measure of the other, and in this movement of reciprocal reference, they impugn each other, yet each founds the other. (Foucault,1972:41)

In this respect Foucault recognizes that psychology represents the tyranny of reason over madness and that it functions within the fabric of civil society itself as opposed to acting solely as an agent of the state. [8] This marks a conceptual difference between Foucault and the Anglo-American tradition of critiques of psychology, the latter viewing psychology purely within the dynamics of state control rather than as a complex structure operating throughout the entirety of society. This Foucualtian conception of the structure of psychology enables it to be formulated, not simply in terms of clinical frameworks and medical institutions, but as a process that has, through transformations and modernizations, led it to include within its sphere a view of what is normal behaviour within society as a whole. For instance, a contemporary example of this is the role the police play in the committing of patients to psychiatric institutions, illustrating psychology's wider functionings. [9] A person may be arrested for causing a disturbance or some other minor offence, but if a criminal act is not committed the police have the option of releasing the subject or, if the disturbance is regularly committed, admitting them to a mental institution. Such institutions provide the police with a mechanism of control that does not depend on the subject perpetrating a criminal act or on a successful prosecution.

Once psychology is located in this wider, social context, it is possible to see how psychology institutionalizes madness. In the words of P Miller, psychology is, "a carceral principle that individualizes madness, the subsequent attempt to medicalize this carceral apparatus, and the psychologization of the insane person." (Miller,1986:37) Foucault's genealogy thus enables the concept of madness to be placed within the wider context of social relations rather than it being just a medical term with limited applications.

With this recognition of the social functions of madness, it is possible to understand why at no point does Foucault attempt to define the concept. He does not view it from the standpoint of rationality, it is not constructed as an unchanging constant entity. Rather, madness is seen in terms of a judgemental concept, a value that is institutionalized as a factual relation. In the preface to *Madness and Civilization* he opens with a quotation from Pascal that exemplifies this: "Men are so necessarily mad, that not to be mad would amount to another form of madness." The term madness is useful for Foucault, as opposed to terms such as insanity or the sick, since it is non-medical, used by everyone and spans the entire time scale with which he is concerned without making any inherent assumptions by its use.

By highlighting the different social functions madness has performed, Foucault opposes a definition of madness that presupposes it to be an unchanging entity that had to wait until the advent of psychology and psychiatry to transform it from a superstitious idea into a scientific concept. This would be advocating an evolutionary teleological view of knowledge; that the object of science exists prior to science itself and is just waiting in the wings to be discovered. Foucault challenges this position throughout his work, arguing that madness is not some eternal concept waiting in an immobile identity for its realization by a positivist science, but it is itself produced by that science in its very act of formulation. The 1% of Parisians who were interned in 1657 were not locked up to rid society of asocial elements, rather the asocial elements were produced by this act of segregation.

Equipped with this term, Foucault takes issue with influential twentieth-century historical analysis of the social functionings of confinement. [10] This position contended that the confinement was a response to economic hardship caused by the changing structure of the means of production. The founding of the Hospital General, Bicetré, Salpêtriéré and other institutions around the late seventeenth century, represented the first large scale internment of people thought to be in some sense deviant. They functioned as prisons, workhouses, asylums and hospitals all in one and this process was seen as a spontaneous elimination of those asocial elements that are now distributed between various modern day institutions. Foucault, however, argues that there are two flaws in this analysis; first to see the movement of confinement as a response to the economic problems of the time is over simplifying and misconstruing the focus of the policy. In his words:

> the relation between the practice of confinement and the insistence on work is not defined by economic considerations; far from it. A moral perception sustains and animates it. When the Board of Trade published its report on the poor in which it proposed the means "to render them useful to the public," it was made quite clear that the origin of poverty was neither scarcity of commodities or unemployment, but "the weakening of discipline and the relaxation of morals". (1965:58-59)

To attempt to reduce this phenomenon of confinement to simple monolithic causes is to misunderstand the complexity of the competing discourses involved. The second flaw in this approach is that it defines madness as an unchanging, historical entity, whereas for Foucault, as stated before, it is a specifically constructed historical entity.

Thus, Foucault saw this phenomenon as a product of a system of thought characteristic of the Classical Age; in which certain traits were regarded as undesirable for both economic and ethical reasons. For instance, the condemnation of idleness resulted in those who did not work being seen as devoid of the social eminence acquired by the community of labour, as Foucault states:

> And it is in this context that the obligation to work assumes its meaning as both ethical exercise and moral guarantee. It will serve as *askesis*, as punishment, as symptom of a certain disposition of the heart. The prisoner who could and who would work would be released, not so much because he was again useful to society, but because he had again subscribed to the greater ethical part of human existence. (1965:59-60)

This attitude towards those who do not work persists to the present day and was prevalent in the Thatcher Government which accorded secondary status to the unemployed. A secondary status that was not solely based on their economic poverty, but also on their apparent lack of a personal stake in the social and ethical structures of society.

It is now possible to fully appreciate the necessity of analysing the historical roots of the subject. Rationality in its modern form emerges in definite circumstances with definite conditions of possibility. This rationality functions within the very fabric of society - not solely as mechanism for state control, but creating the very concepts of definition and formulating them into abstract ideals, ideals that are used to judge and categorize people.

## Criticisms of Foucault

This view of the historical construction of the subject considered above has not gone unchallenged. The final chapter deals with some of the problems and tensions that Foucault's construction of subjectivity creates. However, the crucial criticism considered here is the function and viability of Foucault's historical analysis, since it is the historicity of the subject that is under question in this section.

One of the major criticisms laid at Foucault's door is that he is guilty of presenting an ahistorical analysis of events. [11] As M Poster says when summing up the problems historians have with Foucault's work: "The flow of Foucault's texts, the way one thing is put after another, disturbs the expectations of the reader familiar with social history. There appear to be huge gaps in the narrative, silences that scream at the reader. Topics are annoyingly placed out of the normal order, disrupting one's sense of logical sequence." (Poster,1984:72) In this way Foucault appears to be justifying premises without providing an adequate historical backing.

A proponent of this position is P Sedgwick, (1982) who argues that Foucault merely picks out specific historical data to advance his position without any regard for the historical accuracy or other information that may contradict his arguments. Treatments that Foucault attributes solely to the Age of Reason, Sedgwick argues, were prevalent before and therefore cannot be used to support his analysis of this era, an era which Foucault claims has specific traits and mechanisms of control. Sedgwick advances a different position, that the Age of Reason cannot be seen as historically distinct from other eras because it possesses a continuity with other periods: "What is particularly striking about the long history of psychiatric medicine is its capacity to produce quite different rationalizations for relatively constant practice." (1982:137) As a validation of this continuity he uses the example of water treatment, dunking or submersion, which has been used in various forms throughout the ages.

A possible counter to this position would be to argue that the very rationalization processes behind these "constant practices" is of utmost importance when attempting to elucidate such phenomena. If the rationalizations alter, then the whole meaning and social relevance of the practices is altered. It would be the justifications advanced for various psychiatric treatments that Foucault would be concerned with, not simply focusing on the practices themselves and isolating them from their socio-historical discourse, out of which they are produced.

An effective attack on Foucault's analysis would have to strike at the heart of the purpose and methodology of this history. His methodology cannot be refuted by the tools of conventional historical and scientific discourses because he rejects their criteria for evaluation, and therefore this method is not invalidated merely by demonstrating conflicting examples and specifics. Foucault's analysis is not attempting to perform the same functions as conventional history and it is debatable if it can be characterized as history at all under a rigorous traditional definition. Foucault is an historian of discontinuity and links the unitary rational subject with the historian's ability to provide a continuity of analysis:

> Continuous history is the indispensable correlative of the founding function of the subject: the guarantee that everything that has eluded him will be restored to him; the certainty that time will disperse nothing without restoring it in a reconstituted unity; the promise that one day the subject - in the form of historical consciousness - will once again be able to appropriate, to bring back under his sway, all those things that are kept at a distance by difference, and find in them what might be called his abode. (Foucault,1972:12)

Therefore, all history for Foucault is the product of the time in which it is written, and regardless of the angle from which it was originally conceived, it is analysed in today's terms. No historical analysis can be the true representation of the facts, each historian will distort and privilege certain aspects s/he feels pertinent. However, this is not the crucial point for Foucault; he considers that what is important is the power that this historical knowledge confers on the possessor. As Poster states, the historian, "has an ideological interest in maintaining its importance, reasserting the inevitability with which the past leads to the present, while at the same time denying that there is a certain power at stake." (1984:76) It is this link between knowledge and power that is the salient point in Foucault's analysis. [12]

According to Foucault the dominant scientific discourse has been used as a means of controlling and exerting power over elements in the populace considered to be in need such supervision. Psychology has used the power conferred on it by its scientific status to treat people as it deems necessary, fitting snugly into the dominant power structures, being legitimized and legitimizing. This is the purpose of Foucault's history, to study discontinuity and the operation of power. Under the criteria of conventional historical analysis his work could not be cogent history, but as his aims are wider and very different from the historian it is not possible to dismiss his whole system on such grounds.

Foucault's analysis of madness and psychology has attempted to illustrate both the historical specificity of the term madness and advance a theory of power relations in which psychology operated and exerted influence. In order to develop my argument, that psychology is based on a specific historically constructed definition of human nature, I wish to focus on the discipline itself and analyse how psychology theorizes certain human traits, by developing a case study approach. I want, at the same time, to both provide an example of the functionings of this theory of human nature and to explain the subject's conceptual basis in greater depth.

## Case Study - Racial Prejudice

To illustrate the effects of conceptualizing the subject in an abstract rationalistic form, the work of two leading figures in the study of racial prejudice are examined. In their treatment of prejudice G W Allport (1954 & 1958) and T W Adorno (1950), encapsulate the dominant orthodoxy of social psychology. Following that, *The Scarman Report,* produced after the disturbances in Brixton, will be drawn upon to show the practical consequences of locating racial prejudice at an individual level. Finally, the treatment of Afro-Caribbeans by the psychiatric profession and the discipline of transcultural psychology are considered in order to evaluate the effects such formulations of the subject have on a specific area of psychiatry.

Racial prejudice has been a particularly apposite issue in modern Britain, the way it has been explained and conceptualized and hence the solutions that have been tendered, provide an interesting example of the practical consequences that result from conceiving the social and the individual as two distinct entities. It also provides a useful illustration of the interwoven nature of power structures and the mechanisms by which they operate. Both the way the concept of prejudice has been formulated and the treatment of Afro-Caribbeans within the psychiatric profession are clear manifestations of psychology's unitary rational subject permeating research methodology. This methodology sets psychology on the road to certain conclusions that are made inevitable by the conceptual framework that supports it. In this way the concept of prejudice is constructed in terms of this society. What is defined as racial prejudice applies singularly to experiences in a particular social context; the construction of prejudice is determined by the dominant group using the dominant conceptual frames of reference. Thus, those under consideration, the "ethnic minorities" are studied and analysed with tools that may have very little relevance or meaning to their existence and are judged by criteria that they may find incomprehensible. This leads to a double subjectivity: first, they are objectified by society at large and hence suffer from discrimination; and second, attempts to understand

and rectify this situation of inequality are formulated within the same framework that perpetuates the prejudice in the first instance.

Such a conceptualization of racial prejudice located in the individual-society dichotomy leads to the formulation of certain conclusions concerning the nature, cause, and scope of prejudice. It results in the construction of a concept of racial prejudice that is compatible with existing power relations. First, prejudice is defined in such a way that it locates the area of discrimination on the shoulders of the individual. Second, the notion of the abstract subject has been integral to the production and definition of the very concept of prejudice, enabling it to be seen as an individual affliction. Psychology's construction of subjects leads researchers to regard the social as contingent; not only is racial prejudice an individual phenomenon, but it is the result of the inadequate information-processing mechanism of that individual rather than the effects of outside influences. Thus racial prejudice is a manifestation of deviance and hence irrationality. In this way social structures are not the area for concern, because since institutions are built on rationality, social structures and institutions cannot be inherently prejudiced as to act in a prejudiced fashion would be to manifest irrationally. Therefore it is seen as the individual behaving in an irrational and faulty manner.

The myriad of views that cluster under the umbrella of social psychology can be contrasted with positions that locate prejudice within a wider cultural framework. Under these accounts prejudice is regarded as the product of social and economic factors rather than a failure by specific individuals to realize the irrationality of their position. As M Marable puts it: "Racism, then, is a historically specific concept, which coincided with the unequal racial division of labour within the expansion of capitalist social formulations." (Marable,1985:5) It is important to see racial prejudice as a concept formulated in a social and historical context rather than simply residing in the faulty cognitive processes of the individual. However, it is to these individualistic accounts of prejudice that I will turn.

## Allport and Adorno's Social Psychology

Allport and Adorno are two theorists who have tackled the question of racial prejudice and their work is considered as an example of the treatment the issue receives when located within the framework of the individual-society dichotomy. To pursue this end, the areas of their thought discussed here are those which bear directly on the aforementioned framework. There are obvious differences between the approaches of Allport and Adorno (some of these will be mentioned below); however, the bulk of the analysis is concentrated on the similarities between their work as far as it concerns the individual-society dichotomy.

The work of Allport and Adorno encapsulates the salient premises of social psychology when dealing with attributes that cannot be solely applied  to the individual - attributes that imply some concept of social wholes such as race or class for instance. The ability to see  prejudice as an individual malfunction rests on an empiricist conception of science and the essential dichotomizing of the individual and  society. In order for the theory to work, it is necessary to posit the ideal of an objective  and static reality and this, coupled with a liberal notion of people as essentially equal, forms the bedrock of their analysis of prejudice. It is those who are prejudiced who have difficulty in perceiving  that  people are the same underneath differences of appearance, and their animosity is due to an irrational (and hence incorrect) reading of what is actually around them. Allport and Adorno study prejudice  at  an individual level, that is, focusing on the prejudiced person and the assumptions  behind this position will be developed when considering their arguments.

Both works are based on two fundamental premises; a belief in rationality as an ideal for democratic society and an emphasis on the individual as the area where the breakdown of rationality is  likely  to occur. For Allport rationality and individualism come together to form the basis of science and this is what will provide the stability and cohesion for a democratic society. Scientists are to be responsible for protecting society against subversion and helping people to recognize and overcome irrationality. In Allport's words:

> Democracy, we now realize, places a heavy burden upon the personality, sometimes too great to bear. The maturely democratic person must possess subtle virtues and capacities: an ability to think rationally about causes and effects, an ability to form properly differentiated categories in respect to ethnic groups…it is part of the democratic faith that the objective study of the irrational and immature elements in human behaviour will help us to counteract them. (1954:515)

Allport  constructs rationality and irrationality as two opposing polarities - the democratic society being the exemplary  of  rationality and  the individual as the place where irrationality can be manifested. This breakdown in  rationality  occurs  when  the  individual  does  not perceive true reality - a reality that is embodied within the democratic society.

In certain respects Adorno  formulates a  similar  notion  of the irrational versus the rational. Whereas Allport sought to exclude it from his  main  paradigm,  Adorno uses it as a central feature of his psychoanalytic theory of personality. It is here that  there  lies an important  difference  between  the approaches of the two theorists. Although both theorists locate their analysis of prejudice largely on an individual level, they differ in their treatment of social influence and the areas where  irrationality  will  be  exhibited. Allport considers social influence but simply reduces it to its manifestations in the individual, (1954:Chapter 14) whereas Adorno  leaves greater room in his  theory for some notion of social wholes, although this approach still succumbs to a dualistic construction of the individual and society. In this way, Adorno incorporates a limited analysis of social wholes in his treatment of prejudice and these are brought into play in the guise of socio-ideologies. However, Adorno concentrates on the individual personality as the area where these socio-ideologies will be influencial. His concern is with what type of personality will be susceptible to such ideological constructs, what personality will take on board a fascist dogma when, in a similar situation, others will not:

> The question was,..why is it that certain individuals accept these ideas while other do not?...It was supposed; [1] that anti-semitism probably is not a specific or isolated phenomenon but part of a broad ideological framework, and [2] that an individual's susceptibility to this ideology depends primarily upon his psychological needs. (Adorno,1950:3)

Adorno locates prejudice in a wide socio-ideological historical framework and argues that this is where such prejudice is created, although still looking to an individual level to see where it is exercised and purveyed.

Under this analysis prejudice is the result of a fault in the personality structure of an individual rather than solely a product of interacting with society and socio-ideologies, and it is the breakdown in the individual's rational thought process that will make people susceptible to racist ideologies. To Adorno humans are essentially a reasonable species who, with access to the relevant facts, will make rational judgements and these judgements will not be prejudiced ones. He speaks out strongly against theories which rebuke this view, as without it,

> we would have to share the destructive view, which has gained some acceptance in the modern world, that since all ideologies, all philosophies, derive from non-rational sources there is no basis for saying that one has more merit than another. (1950:11)

The object of Adorno's study is to make people more reasonable by knowing the psychological determinants of ideology. When the phenomenon of Nazism is evaluated, Adorno concludes that the appeal of fascism could not have been a result of a rationally-based decision by the populace because Nazism did not serve the real interests of the people. In this way: "It must therefore make its major appeal, not to rational self-interest, but to emotional needs - often to the most primitive and irrational wishes and fears." Thus the study, once the debate has been framed in these terms, must concentrate on personality: "why are people so easily fooled? Because, it may be supposed, of their personality structure." (1950:10) and this, "personality structure may be

80

such as to render the individual susceptible to anti-democratic propaganda." (1950:7)

Adorno's work slips easily into dualism, constructing an antagonism between the individual and society. Further, he builds on this and considers society and its influences solely in reference to the effects on the individual, and thus privileges the individuals role. Although ideological factors clearly influence the person, the study and evaluation of prejudice should be done primarily at an individual level, because this is where the underlying causes lie:

> The research to be reported in this volume was guided by the following major hypothesis: that the political, economic, and social convictions of an individual often form a broad and coherent pattern, as if bound together by a "mentality" or "spirit", and that this pattern is an exposition of deep-lying trends in his personality. (1950:1)

These deep-lying trends in personality structure are studied by the traditional, scientific methods of experimental psychology: "The clinical studies gave access to the deeper personality factors behind anti-democratic ideology and suggested means for their investigation on a large scale." (1950:13) Consequently, Adorno employs a method for observing these traits consisting of questionnaires containing factual questions and opinion-attitude scales for determining the authoritarian personality. By this careful evaluation of the individual's personality it will be possible to analyse prejudice scientifically against a uniform standard of rational behaviour.

Adorno recognized that these scientific methods could not provide the whole answer to the problem of prejudice as the causes are complex and deep-rooted: "It seems obvious therefore that the modification of the potentially fascist structure cannot be achieved by psychological means alone....These are products of the total organisation of society and are to be changed only as that society is changed." (1950:10) Even though the study makes several passing references to society and the universal structures that affect certain susceptible personality structures in their development, Adorno concludes that even if social reforms were passed or the structure of society changed prejudice could still prevail. These reforms would not change the personality structures of the individual and it is here that the locus of causation lies:

> We believe that the scientific understanding of society must include an understanding of what it does to people, and that it is possible to have social reforms, even broad and sweeping ones, which though desirable in their own right would not necessarily change the structure of the prejudiced personality. (1950: 975-6)

Adorno is able to reach this conclusion by postulating prejudice as a concept that operates by appealing to the irrational mentality of the individual. It does not appeal to real self-interests, in fact it can go against them, its attraction operates on an appeal to emotions. Social ideologies that promote discrimination will appeal to certain personality structures and in this way prejudice will be perpetuated. Although it is not Adorno's explicit aim to locate prejudice and its causation solely on an individual level, his methodology and conceptual framework necessitate such an outcome. His clinical methodology reveals only the attitudes and opinions of individuals and the conceptual framework that sees prejudice as a doctrine that appeals to certain personality structures ultimately puts the debate into an individualistic structure.

Allport shared Adorno's concern for the individual, and constructed methods to quantify these individual attitudes. The main impact of his work was his use of a social attitude paradigm - seeing the study of attitudes as the key to behaviour, rather than focusing on behavioural manifestation. With this methodology Allport formulated two approaches that proved fruitful in the study of individual attitudes:

> In the longitudinal approach the investigator attempts to trace back through a given life history factors that might account for the present pattern of prejudice....The cross-sectional method attempts to find out what the contemporary prejudice pattern is like, asking especially how ethnic attitudes are related to other social attitudes and to one's outlook in general. (1954:395)

The aim of this approach was to bridge the gap between the individual and society, looking at the individual but determining social factors by the answers that would be received. Instead, the effect of this approach was to reinforce the individual-society divide, reducing the fundamental cause of prejudice in an individual to faulty information-processing mechanisms, as opposed to the rationalist ideal of an undistorted judgement. This emphasis on individual attitudes and quantification has now become the basic methodology of much modern social psychology.

Allport combines two approaches when studying prejudice: the stimulus-object approach which emphasizes the subject (the prejudiced person) seeing, "bona fide differences", (1954:85-86) or causes for their prejudice; and the phenomenological approach which analyzes the area where the representation of the object is not directly perceived but comes from the wider views of the person. Under this account, Allport discusses,

> at considerable length the process of perceiving and cognizing group differences. This focusing of cognition upon the stimulus-object is sometimes called the *"phenomenological"* level of study. The prejudiced *"act"* depends on the way the stimulus-object is perceived (ie its phenomenology). (1954:206)

These approaches operate within the context of Allport's essential dualism and one that legitimizes the idea of racial prejudice that is found in a common-sense understanding - prejudiced people incorrectly perceive differences when there are none.

With this methodology Allport is able to infer that the cognitive processes of prejudiced people are different from those of non-prejudiced ones. (1954:217) He makes links between these attitudes and the other perceptions an individual may have about the world. For instance, Allport cites a study of anti-semitic women students and comes to the following conclusions, "Prejudice is frequently woven firmly into a style of life." (1958:372) And he gives some examples of the differences that might be exhibited between prejudiced and non-prejudiced people:

> The anti-semitic girls had more fantasies of their parents' deaths....Strict insistence on cleanliness, good manners, conventions is more common among them than among tolerant people. When asked the question, "What is the most embarrassing experience?" anti-semitic girls responded in terms of violations of mores and conventions in public. Whereas non-prejudiced girls spoke more often of inadequacy of personal relations, such as failing to live up to a friend's expectations. (1958:374-5)

Allport then complies a list of traits that the prejudiced person will demonstrate:

> Ambivalence towards parents.
> Moralism.
> Dichotomization.
> A need for definiteness
> Externalization of conflict
> Institutionalization.
> Authoritarianism. (1958:374)

This location of prejudice as an affliction of the individual precludes other ways of analysing racism (for example seeing it as a product of socio-economic forces). This leads to the view that only a few misguided people are prejudiced and it is not a widespread or particularly dangerous threat to society. Thus prejudice becomes error - an error in the cognitive processes of an individual. In order for this approach to work, the democratic society has to embody the correct, rational perception of group differences. Under a liberal democratic formulation these differences should not affect the rights or treatment of minority groups.

It can be seen that Allport and Adorno conceptualize prejudice as an attribute that can only, by definition, apply to an individual. Allport conceives contemporary democratic society as the bastion of rational and scientific ideals. A prejudiced individual in this context will be exhibiting irrational and "wrong" tendencies, tendencies that can be corrected if s/he is given the right information to redress their faulty perceptions. Adorno also argues for the irrationality of prejudice, seeing it as something that appeals to the emotions and uninformed urges of individuals. Under both these accounts, in which prejudice is so formulated that social institutions could not themselves be prejudiced, it is hard to see how social factors can be brought into play. This would be possible only in so far as they are made up of individuals who hold these opinions. The central flaw in these accounts is the reliance on the notion of prejudice as an irrational act, an act that goes against the inherent rationality of a democratic society. It could be argued that to be prejudiced in this society is in fact to act rationally, as it would be following the direction of certain institutions. These institutions, although they are supposed to be rational, can and do exhibit prejudice, for example the police force or recent legislation on immigration. This point will be developed further when *The Scarman Report* is considered and in the analysis of Afro-Caribbeans' experiences in psychiatry.

## *The Social Categorization Approach*

These mechanisms of social psychology provide the conceptual basis for the socio-cognitive accounts of prejudice that will now be considered. This socio-cognitive account is discussed to illustrate what the logical conclusion to the individualist trends mentioned above can be in modern psychology. The treatment is therefore brief, simply making the point that a location of prejudice at an individual level, as a manifestation of irrationality, results in social psychology concentrating solely on the individual. Thus prejudice is examined by conducting clinical experiments to determine these manifestations.

H Tajfel, a leading proponent of this methodology, (1971) formulated the Social Categorization Approach (SCA), based on a laboratory-orientated experimental method. This approach looks at the role of cognitive processes in intergroup differences, as Tajfel states:

> In the present experiments it was shown that a social categorization into groups based explicitly on a criterion of randomness led to behaviour which differentiated more clearly the ingroup from the outgroup than was the case for a categorization based on a non-random interindividual similarity. (1971:49-50)

Despite Tajfel's shift from perception to cognition as the principal element of study, the basic assumptions of the former are not altered, namely, that correct information-processing, that is, a rational and objective process, would produce an accurate representation. The SCA rigidly adhered to a scientific methodology using controlled laboratory experiments in which value and meaning were seen as complex variables that had to be controlled in order to achieve coherent results.

As a result of their controlled experiments, (1971:50) Tajfel concluded that prejudice was a result of cognitive error, a discrepancy between the perception of the prejudiced person and that of the scientist. The analysis rests, as does Allport's and Adorno's, on conceptualizing prejudice as an error. The limitations of such an approach become apparent when the analysis is applied to social phenomena as opposed to purely cognitive processes like memory. Any meaningful criteria such as value judgements are necessarily excluded and it is here problems arise. Inadvertently social psychologists change the grounds of their argument; although the experimental method is alleged to provide a scientific evaluation of prejudice, their initial premise that racial prejudice is wrong is surely a value judgement, a value judgement that no scientific method could reveal, making it unlikely that prejudice could be analysed by such a method. The notion of error in categorizing a concept such as prejudice is inherently problematic for social psychology, as errors are by definition exceptions as opposed to rules, and it is difficult to see how such errors can be responsible for common everyday behaviour within our society.

## The Scarman Report

The effects of conceptualizing racial prejudice as an individual phenomenon which by definition cannot reside in social institutions are lucidly illustrated by the findings of *The Scarman Report* (1981). Lord Scarman investigated the riots that took place in 1981 and attempted to analyse their cause. *The Scarman Report* provides an useful example of how commonsense understanding of prejudice (a perception of unwarranted difference), upon which social psychology is based, results in certain answers being put forward and others marginalized. Hence, *The Scarman Report* was able to locate the cause of the riots as racial prejudice - not racial prejudice of the police force as an institution, but the racial prejudice of individual officers:

> The direction of the Metropolitan Police is not racist. I totally and unequivocally reject the attack made upon the integrity and impartiality of the senior direction in the force. The criticism lies elsewhere - in errors of judgement, in a lack of imagination and flexibility, but not in deliberate bias or prejudice. The allegation that the police are the oppressive arm of a racist state not only displays a complete ignorance of the constitutional arrangements for controlling the police: it is an injustice to the senior officers of the force. (1981:4.62)

In this way, it was due: "Sadly to the ill-considered, immature and racially prejudiced actions of some officers in their dealings on the street with young black people." (1981:4.63) This puts the blame not on the police force as an institution, but on one or two misguided officers and probably from the lower ranks: "I am satisfied that such bias (against black people) is not to be found amongst senior officers." (1981:4.63)

The nature of the prejudice is individualized. It is not to be found in the police force nor indeed in state bodies, as these institutions cannot be founded on ignorance and irrationality, the two forces which, Scarman argues, generate prejudice. The very perception of the police by the local community is also subject to the distorting effects of irrationality: "In Brixton even one isolated instance of misconduct can foster a whole legion of rumours which rapidly become beliefs firmly held within the community. Whether justified or not, many in Brixton believe the police routinely abuse their powers." (1981:4.67) Consequently, both the behaviour of the "few" policemen and the community is seen as irrationally based. The policemen are irrational in their prejudice against black people and the community are ignorant of the police as their knowledge is confined to beliefs and rumours. Although he acknowledges that police harassment of individuals may take place, Scarman argues that most of the complaints are exaggerated because: "The position may almost have been reached where not to do so is to endanger one's credibility in the eyes of one's friends." (1981:4.60)

He firmly rejects the claim that Britain is an institutionally racist society, "if by that it is meant that it is a society which knowingly, as a matter of policy, discriminates against black people, I reject that allegation." (1981:2.22) An institution such as the police force cannot be built on irrationality and hence cannot be said to be prejudiced. *The Scarman Report* gives a clear indication of how the conceptual framework of social psychology necessitates certain conclusions, enabling the inquiry to provide a formulation of racial prejudice that is compatible with the concurrent ideology of the state and with existing power relations. Prejudice seen in this way is just a misdemeanour by isolated individuals, one that can be laid at the door of individuals both in the police force and the community. [13]

## Psychiatry and minorities

Once the structures of social psychology have been examined, it is illuminating to analyse the practical results and applications of this theorizing. The conceptual framework that governs the discussion of prejudice is taken by psychiatry and incorporated into its diagnostic criteria when dealing with "ethnic minorities". The individual-society dichotomy inherent in social psychology's approach to racial prejudice affects the treatment of Afro-Caribbeans within British psychiatry, localizing afflictions to an individual level of breakdown and failing to take into consideration the wider social factors that will influence and even create such difficulties. To illustrate these claims the discipline of transcultural psychology will be considered, a discipline that seeks to redress the unacceptable treatment of Afro-Caribbeans by psychiatry and take into account their cultural background during diagnostic procedure.

Research done in the 1970s and 1980s [14] shows conclusively that Afro-Caribbeans are over-represented among psychiatric patients. This conclusion raises several issues. The first concerns the numbers in psychiatric hospitals; the second issue concerns how and why they got there and the relationship between the law and psychiatry in the admission procedure; and the third issue is one of diagnosis, that is whether Afro-Caribbeans are more likely to suffer from mental illness or whether the very diagnostic process is at fault. The issue of diagnosis or misdiagnosis is of crucial importance when analysing the subject of race in psychiatry and it will be considered here as a crucial factor in an evaluation of transcultural psychology, a discipline that attempts to reconstruct the premises of conventional psychiatry. Both strands of psychiatry, conventional and transcultural, are criticized on the grounds that they retain the notion of an individual-centred analysis in which the individual is the main site of any disintegration or anomaly.

The discipline of transcultural psychology has grown up in an attempt to understand and respond to the disproportionate Afro-Caribbean presence in Britain's mentally ill population. In order to do this, a concept of culture has to be formulated so that one can begin to explain the different behavioural patterns and frames of reference. The central task of this approach is to locate mental illness within a wider context by putting it in a cultural and socially specific framework, rather than seeing mental illness as an objective monolithic phenomenon. In the words of C Ranger:

> The traditional view of medical knowledge, as distinct from medical practice, has been that it is independent of social forces. The basic assumption of those involved in medical research, practice and teaching has been that medical knowledge deals with facts about the human body and mind, and the diseases which can afflict them. These facts are seen to exist independently of the observer. (Ranger, 1989:357)

A critique of this traditionalist position can be illustrated by looking at an outline of the aims and objectives of the Transcultural Psychiatry Society:

> The aims of the society are to initiate and sustain interest in transcultural psychiatry, to increase awareness and understanding of the effects of culture upon health and illness; and to encourage practitioners to develop sensitivity to the cultural values, skills and systems of thought by which people organise their lives, including in particular, the factors which are most relevant to mental illness. (Constitution of the Transcultural Society, 1976)

Accordingly, Littlewood and Lipsedge, major exponents of transcultural psychiatry, begin their inquiry into racism within psychiatry by locating it at the door of traditional scientific methodology, this necessitates the conclusion:

Not merely has science legitimized racialism in certain particulars, but the whole nature of the scientific enterprise has perhaps contributed to its possibility. The fragmentary, empirical nature of our theorizing leads to that split between idea and feeling which was carried to its conclusion in Auschwitz or in the slave trade; legal argument long centred on whether non-Europeans should be treated as people or as objects. (Littlewood & Lipsedge,1982:54)

The culmination of this approach is the placing of transcultural psychiatry in the wider tradition of social constructionism, [15] aiming to reject traditional notions of scientific objectivity and diseases as pre-existent of human inquiry.

More specifically, the use of culture as an analytic tool can be seen in Littlewood and Lipsedge's work when they call into question the validity of diagnostic procedures when applied to Afro-Caribbeans. For instance, when they compared the symptoms of Afro-Caribbean patients with the conventional descriptions of schizophrenia it was found that a very small percentage conformed to the usual model. [17] Afro-Caribbean patients were also more likely to have their diagnosis changed during their stay in institutions, indicating an uncertainty among the psychiatrists as to what exactly was wrong with the patient. Littlewood and Lipsedge put forward a new clinical term to explain the symptoms of the West Indian patients, "acute psychotic reaction", and consequently, "the increase in the diagnosis of schizophrenia in the West Indian born may be due in part to the occurrence of acute psychotic reactions which are diagnosed as schizophrenia." (Littlewood,1981)

Littlewood and Lipsedge argue that British psychiatrists fail to recognize the meaning of Afro-Caribbeans' behaviour because they have no knowledge of the cultural context from which it stems. What is in fact a temporary breakdown caused by the social stress of living in a hostile society may be interpreted as the symptoms of schizophrenia. The practitioner unaware of these factors will be unable to form a considered diagnosis and therefore construe such symptoms within his/her own frame of reference. For instance, religious and supernatural beliefs can produce symptoms of delusion or hallucination but are not the manifestations of schizophrenia. In the words of Aggrey Irons, the senior medical officer at Bellevue Hospital, Kingston, Jamaica:

People talk about black magic, people talk about witch doctors in negative terms, and if someone is experiencing a hard time it is very easy for them to externalize that, and say, someone out there is doing something to me....Tie it altogether and you get some really good first rank symptoms of schizophrenia. (Horizon,1989)

Casting spells or being cursed, in the context of contemporary British culture, are bizarre and unusual activities. But once put in the context of another culture where they are part of the normal framework of discourses, which is collective and social in nature, they no longer seem so odd. The Western-trained psychiatrists can easily misinterpret utterances and actions if they have no knowledge of the patient's culture. Transcultural psychiatry aims to correct this ethnocentricity by making practitioners aware of the cultural specificity of these outbursts which are so peculiar to the British eye. Such a policy could redress the diagnostic imbalance, but there are further factors that affect the treatment of "ethnic minority" patients.

Not only is their culture misunderstood, it is bracketed with anti-social and deviant acts. As Ballard states: "It is easy to slip...into regarding distinctive minority cultural patterns themselves as being problematic and pathological." (Ballard,1979:162) The white practitioner perceives from the outset the Afro-Caribbean patient's culture as a problem and such an initial premise will impede understanding. Ballard goes on to say, "it is all too easy to slip into a perception of the cultural worlds of others as an irrational product of sheer ignorance. Action based on such premises does no more than demonstrate the social power of the practitioner." (Ballard,1979:162) This highlights another dimension in the relationship between the practitioner and patient; not only is the practitioner ignorant of the patient's culture, the patient is stereotyped and characterized as a problem simply because s/he is from a different background. These factors illustrate how the psychiatric profession can operate in a prerogative fashion, creating the pathologization of the ethnic community so that they become by definition mentally ill - to exhibit personality traits formed in another culture is a problem in itself.

Transcultural psychiatry aims to overcome these problems and diagnostic biases by opening up a dialogue of understanding and a comprehension of different cultures. The worth of such work is obvious and the major contribution is the introduction of a recognition of culturally mediated expression in the process of diagnosis. This highlights the roles of social and cultural factors instead of relying on a purely biological construction of mental illness and problems. Transcultural psychiatry is only the first step towards redressing the ethnocentricity of psychiatry itself; this analysis needs to be extended and developed. The position also relies too heavily on the use of culture as an analytic tool, a knowledge of a patient's culture is not enough to change the discriminatory practices in diagnosis.

By their use of the notion of culture in the diagnosis procedure, Littlewood and Lipsedge could create a difficult situation for British psychiatry. If it is the prejudice of the society at large that causes Afro-Caribbeans to suffer stress and anxiety that would not be found in white people to the same extent, then, it is not only that Afro-Caribbeans' problems are caused by the system, but they have to be treated by the same system that caused the problem in the first place. Consequently, the

Afro-Caribbean's experience becomes doubly distorted; first, by the dominant culture and second, by psychiatry, which becomes a moulding process, a form of punishment for not conforming to the dominant modes of behaviour. This power relation is one of psychiatry's major functions. It operates within society to control and punish forms of behaviour that do not conform to the prevalent model. Thomas Szasz makes the point that different traits are problematized in different eras: "Throughout the nineteenth century masturbation was regarded as a cause and symptom of insanity." (Szasz,1979:xvi) Nowadays within psychology masturbation is no longer regarded as an exposition of insanity, thus illustrating how pathological traits are relative to social circumstance and time.

There are two fundamental flaws in the reasoning of transcultural psychiatry and these create obstacles to its success: first, the reliance on the practitioner as the site for change; and second, the retention of disease categories and medicine's scientific status. The first point is illustrated by examining the area where transcultural psychiatry concentrates its analysis. Ballard, for instance, argues that the solution to the problem of race in psychiatry consists of providing more information for the white practitioner about different cultures, the crucial area is the relationship between the patient and the practitioner. In the words of K Mercer: "The point of application of the transcultural project is narrowed down to the space between doctor and patient. This relationship is the site on which problem and solution are posed in terms of culture, knowledge and communication." (Mercer,1986:131) This is the result of a definition of racial prejudice that locates it as a fault in the information-processing mechanism of the individual. It is an irrational position and can be corrected by providing knowledge to redress the ignorance. Accordingly, the proper site for the alleviation of prejudice is the individual - the practitioner in this case. Clearly, simply providing greater information and training practitioners will not eradicate the problem completely. It relies too heavily on the individual practitioner responding positively to these intiatives and makes no provision for those who do not.

The second point, which is crucial for transcultural psychiatry, is one that so far has been considered only in passing. Transcultural psychiatry must challenge the scientific objectivity of conventional psychiatry and reformulate disease categories. To locate prejudice as an affliction of the practitioner and give no analysis of the structures that perpetuate the discrimination results in the fundamental problem remaining unsolved, just a papering over of cracks. Disease categories must be put in their social and cultural context,[17] so they can be viewed as specific not timeless entities.

It has been seen that social psychology's definition of racial prejudice is implicitly assimilated into modern transcultural psychiatry. This tacit acceptance of an individualist definition of prejudice, that sees it as a deviation from the rational norm and an inadequate challenge to the hegemony of scientific medicine, are the twin conceptual flaws that hinder a radical reformulation of psychiatry. The terrible consequences for those at the receiving end of "treatments" legitimized by this conceptual framework is a consideration that must not be ignored in the complexities of the abstract debate.

## Conclusion

From the preceding analysis it is possible to see how the subject was formulated in a specific historical and social context; it was constructed to perform a function in a changing world which needed differing values and attitudes from the previous era. New economic developments altered the structure of work and leisure and the rational conception of man fitted into these new patterns. The old world view of man's place in nature ordained by a God would not have provided a satisfactory basis for capitalism. People needed to be able to aspire to change and advancement through hard work; rationality could be learned and acquired, unlike God-given traits. Not only this, individualism encouraged people to see themselves as discrete units, rather than as part of a community and this furthered the ethos of capitalism, people now worked for their own individual benefit, without recourse to the wider community or the long term effects that this could have on the environment. At the same time a conflicting strand of thought was equally prevalent: that human nature was biologically determined and man had evolved into what he was. This biological base was conceptualized by Darwinian theory in which reason became naturalized. These seemingly conflicting ideas concerning the roots of human nature could operate in perfect harmony in one society. If society is conceived as a web of discourses, each performing different functions but supporting the same whole, conflicting ideologies within one system do not have to be viewed as problematic. All societies operate as a mesh of contradictions and these discourses only make sense once they are looked at in their entirety.

The chapter has closely examined the inadequacy and problems of the rationalistic subject; the next chapter looks at the arguments for a new formulation of the subject, considering various attempts to construct an alternative formulation of human nature and subjectivity.

# Notes

1. The discussion of the scientific revolution will be brief as there have been many excellent treatments of the issue, for example see: Hill,C. (1975), *Reformation to Industrial Revolution,* Pelican, Harmondsworth. Easlea,B. (1980), *Witchhunting, Magic and the New Philosophy,* Harvester, Brighton. Merchant,C. (1979), *The Death of Nature: women, ecology, and the scientific revolution,* Harper & Row, London. Merchant,C. & Dijksterhuis,E,J. (1961), *The Mechanization of the World Picture,* Clarendon Press. Bridenthal,R. & Koony,C. (1977), (ed.), *Becoming Visible,* Houghton Mifflin, Boston.

2. For example see experiments done by E Weber & G Fechner that aimed to clarify the structure of sensory organs and establish the relation between the quality of sensory experience and the physical characteristics of their stimulus. In Capra,F. (1987), *The Turning Point,* Flamingo, London.

3. See: Canguilhem. (1975), "Physics of the External Senses", *Etudes d histoire et de Philosophie des Sciences*, Paris, Vrin.

4. See Chapter Four for an elaboration of Foucault's theory of the subject. Venn's article is not criticized here as she builds so heavily on a Foucaultian framework that the critique of Foucault in the later sections will serve as a critique of her work.

5. See: Mackie, J.L. (1982), *The Miracle of Theism,* Oxford University Press, Oxford.

6. For a classic example of this type of work see: Young,M & Willmott,P. (1962), *Family and Kinship in East London,* Pelican, Harmondsworth.

7. See the discussion on bio-power in Chapter Four.

8. For similar positions see: Castel,F. (1976), *L Ordre Psychiatrique,* Paris Editions de Minuit. Dorner,K. (1981), *Madmen & the Bourgeoisie,* Basil Blackwell, Oxford.

9. For instance, the compulsory admittance to mental hospitals under Section 136 of the 1983 Mental health act is non-criminal legislation that the police can invoke as a controlling measure.

10. See: Foucault. (1965), *Madness & Civilization,* and Sheridan,A. (1980), *Michel Foucault: The will to truth,* Tavistock Publications, London. page 25.

11. For a extensive history of madness see: Bynum,R. Porter,R. & Shepherd,M. (ed.), (1988), *The Anatomy of Madness: essays in the history of psychiatry, Volume three: The asylum and its psychiatry,* Routledge, London. This provides evidence that could be said to contradict the Foucaultian analysis, in the words of H.Freeman, the editors claim that, "the evolution of the asylum "led to the emergence of the wider psycho-politics concerned with the place of abnormality within society." Perhaps it should have done, but all the evidence here is that it didn't." Freeman.H, review of *Volume Three,* in the *Times Higher Educational Supplement,* 11/8/89. p19.

12. See Foucault,M. (1980), *Power/Knowledge: selected interviews & other writings,* 1972-77, Gordon,C. (ed.), Pantheon Books, New York.

13. As a contrast to the *Scarman Report* see: (1986), *The Broadwater Farm Inquiry,* (with an introduction by Lord Gifford Q.C.), Karia Press, London.

14. See: Cochrane,R. (1977), "Mental illness in immigrants to England & Wales", *Social Psychiatry,* 12. For studies done in Birmingham, McGovan,D. & Cope,R,V. (1987), "First Psychiatric admissions rates of first & second generation Afro-Caribbeans", *Social Psychiatry,* 22. In Nottingham, Harrison,G. et al., "A prospective study of Severe Mental Disorder in Afro-Caribbean patients", in *Psychological Medicine,* 18, (3).

15. See the collection edited by Mishler,E.G. et al. (1981), *Social Contexts of Health, Illness, & Patient Care,* Cambridge University Press, Cambridge.

16. See Mercer,K. (1986), "Racism & transcultural psychiatry", in Miller & Rose (ed.), *The Power of Psychiatry,* Polity Press, London.

17. See: Ranger (1989).

# 4 Towards a new definition of the subject

## Introduction

This chapter is concerned with new ideas about the subject and attempts to think beyond the conventional frameworks towards alternative conceptions. First, the work of the Indian philosopher Krishnamurti is examined. He casts the subject in a much more dynamic and relational role than traditional formulations of the subject and attempts to overcome what he perceives as the damaging dualism between the individual and society. Second, Foucault's subject is considered: he constructs the subject as an historically constituted entity, enmeshed in a web of discourses, a theory that runs counter to the traditional humanist view of individuality. Third, criticisms of Foucault's subject, namely the claim that it could lead to a relativist position, are examined showing how he can overcome such a relativist dilemma and build a useful analysis of the subject's formulation. Finally, how these new ideas of subjectivity circumvent some of the problems created by the traditional abstract individual are mentioned. These points are illustrated by showing how the dichotomy between the individual and society is problematized by these new subjects and how a better relationship between the two terms can be made possible.

The inclusion of Krishnamurti and Foucault in the same chapter is not intended to imply that they are advocating similar or compatible positions. However, both theorists have two commonalities, which are first, a dissatisfaction with the abstract individual as a definition of humanity and second, a recognition of the socio-political effects of such definitions. The routes they choose to overcome these problems are, nevertheless, conceptually dissimilar and indicate that there is not necessarily one solution to the problems of subject construction.

In the previous chapters there have been long discussions concerning the problems created by an abstract unitary conception of the subject and the resulting effects this has for social theory. This chapter turns to the issue of how these problems can be overcome; what formulations of the subject could circumvent the previously mentioned tensions. Before this project commences two points must be mentioned: first, this analysis does not claim to be a definitive solution to the conceptual exclusivity of the terms "the individual" and "society": it is only a tentative first step in a re-conception of the subject. Second, in this creation of a new conception of the subject, the problems and difficulties of the conventional formulation will grow clearer and its defects more saliently highlighted. Therefore, this analysis has the twin aims of starting on a journey to a more adequate and useful subject formulation and further elucidating the difficulties of the old. At this stage a complete and watertight theory of the new subject is not on the agenda, it is enough that it fulfils the previously mentioned aims. [1]

Chapter Two discussed the conceptual problems that collectivism inherited from individualism, viz: an adherence to a pre-given subject and the central position this subject occupies in social theory. In this sense the two doctrines (individualism and collectivism) share their conceptual legacy: both arose out of the same social framework [2] and both have been used to support one another in a reciprocal fashion. This point is made by Iris Young when she discusses methods to overcome the alienation and individualism of modern Western society. Traditionally, a notion of "community" or "collectivity" had been formulated to replace individualism and surmount the problems the latter produces - yet these collective ideas may be so linked to individualism that they cannot provide an alternative way forward:

> Like most such oppositions, moreover, individualism and community have a common logic underlying their polarity, which makes it possible for them to define each other negatively. Each entails a denial of difference and desire to bring multiplicity and heterogeneity into unity, though in opposing ways. Liberal individualism denies difference by positing the self as a solid, self-sufficient unity, not defined by or in need of anything or anyone other than itself. Its formalistic ethic of rights denies difference by levelling all such separated individuals under a common measure of rights. Community, on the other hand, denies difference by positing fusion rather than separation as the social ideal. Community proponents conceive the social subject as a relation of unity composed by identification and symmetry among individuals within a totality. (Young,1990:307)

By underwriting each other's claims individualism and collectivism are mutually supporting. "The neat distinction between individualism and community thus generates a dialectic in which each is a condition for the other." (Young,1990:307) Both doctrines were created out of the same epistemological framework, a framework based on the rationalist and totalizing theories that date back to the Enlightenment. Individualism patently ignores something that clearly exists, namely an amalgamation of individual wants, aims and structures - in other words society. And since this society produces effects and influences individuals, it is an essential area of study. An epistemological framework that has no place for something as pertinent as societal factors would not last long as an exposition of reality. Therefore, individualism needs another theory such as collectivism to maintain its hegemony. Between them, the two doctrines will provide coverage of all aspects of social organization, and within this epistemological system the one-dimensional analysis of individualism will not be so glaring an omission; collectivism will be there to consider the areas individualism cannot accommodate in its conceptual structures.

The epistemological framework was so structured that it was able to incorporate both the individual and society into the frames of analysis, but unfortunately by positioning them as contrarieties it produced an inadequate conception of each entity. There are two things that manifestly exist when looking around: individual people, and the groups in which they live. No philosophy of humanity could feasibly ignore either the individual or society, so the solution within the Western dualist traditional was to construct two polarities and erect two theories around them. In this way no visible facet of social life was ignored and social criticism could proceed. Humanity and its organizations were divided into two parts, which were cast as distinct entities, just as the mind and body had been similarly separated. The split in these cases mirrors the fundamental split between spirit and matter. The mind and society corresponded to the spiritual side of the divide. They were regarded as intangible entities that could not be touched, seen or felt, but nevertheless seemed to exist in some influential and important form. On the other hand, the body and the individual corresponded to the material. They were tangible entities that could be touched, seen and heard, and which there could be no argument over their existence itself, only argument over the type of existence that could be said to pertain to them.

These contrasting divisions in theory could simply have been useful tools of clarification and study, but in practice they resulted in the inability to resynthesize these two entities. For instance, once the person had been divided into the twin components of mind and body, the resynthesis of the two components became theoretically fraught with tensions due to the conceptual structures that had been erected around them. The formulation of any social influence on the individual is similarly fraught. There is a difficulty in how the non-tangible society effects change on the tangible individual. This is a problem for both individualism and collectivism. Just as individualism suffers from a neglect of society and its influences, collectivism can be accused of the reverse process: although society is said to be made up of many individuals, it takes on its own dynamic in collective analysis that subjugates the individual's position and makes interaction between the two very difficult.

This is the legacy for social theory and these dichotomies create the subject of this discipline, enabling the individual to occupy a central

96

place in analysis and retain an individualistic notion of a predetermined entity: these are the two facets to which a new conception of the subject must address itself. In this way separate notions of the individual and society could be destroyed (or highly problematized) by a new dynamic view of the subject, and such a project could form a deeper and more sustained critique of the dichotomy between the individual and society.

There are two separate points in this new formulation that need to be clarified; there is a difference between the goals of reconstructing the subject and reappraising its central role in social theory. In many ways the former is an attempt to postulate a new theory of human nature. This new theory of human nature has to find an alternative to constructing the subject as a pre-given entity. The latter is a reorganization of social theory, so it could tolerate a new entity as its object under study, an institution or structure for example. That is not to say the reconstructing of the subject will not have huge repercussions for the ability of social theory to put the subject in a central role, since this relies to a large extent on the subject construed as a pre-given entity, thus capable of always fitting into its allotted slot. Suffice to say it is important to recognize that the two problems created by the dichotomy do not necessarily have identical solutions.

## Krishnamurti and the Subject

A useful direction to take in the initial stages of reconstructing the subject is to look at the way such issues are dealt with in Eastern philosophy. Unfortunately, space does not allow for a full-scale appraisal of an Eastern conception of human nature, so the account will concentrate on the work of one of the best known Indian philosophers, Krishnamurti. His conception of human nature can be used to illustrate a different idea of humanity to the one prevalent in the West. It is in its capacity as a window into another world of ideas that this example is used, simply to show that there can be alternative notions of humanity, notions that are distinct from the ones we have become accustomed to see as necessarily and naturally true, rather than as a concrete definitional construction of the subject.

Krishnamurti's approach to the study of the subject is radically different from Western ideas of social inquiry. The differences are most clearly marked in respect to the analysis of social explanation and subject formulation put forward by individualism. It is difficult to discuss certain Eastern ideas using the English language and relying solely on the written word to communicate, as so much of Eastern philosophy is a practical endeavour. With these limitations, and the use I want to make of Krishnamurti's subject, in mind certain omissions are inevitable. Consequently, Krishnamurti's treatment of the subject is considered, not, however, his wider philosophical aims. Therefore the aspects of his subject that are discussed are those which are informative and useful for the project in hand, rather than an account of his views in their entirety.

In Krishnamurti's analysis the individual is neither elevated to primary importance nor subjugated by the notion of society. Along with Western individualism the unit Krishnamurti addresses is the individual, but the consequences of this concentration on an individual level are very different from those that Western individualists infer. Krishnamurti conceives of the individual and society as linked together in the form of a relationship, and further, the relationship between one person and another is what constitutes society. The link between the individual and society is such that, if a person is confused and chaotic within that, by projection, becomes the world and therefore society. The type of society we live in is not created by some form of abstract political ideology, or by others who control us, but by ourselves as much as anyone else. When looking at the causes of misery and confusion, Krishnamurti says:

> You and I have created it, not a capitalist nor a communist nor a fascist society, but you and I have created it in our relationship with each other. What you are within has been projected without, on to the world; what you are, what you think and what you feel, what you do in your everyday existence, is projected outwardly, and that constitutes the world. (Krishmamurti,1987:16)

Under Krishnamurti's formulation the world's problems are the individual's problems and vice versa. This is due to Krishnamurti's premise that it is essentially the relationships people form that create society or, rather, these relationships are the definition of society. It is up to the individual to improve these personal relationships and then global change can be affected. In order to facilitate this:

> we must begin near, that is we must concern ourselves with our daily existence, with our daily thoughts and feelings and actions which are revealed in the manner of earning our livelihood and in our relationship with ideas or beliefs. This is our daily existence, is it not? We are concerned with getting jobs, earning money; we are concerned with the relationship with our family or with our neighbours, and we are concerned with ideas and with beliefs. (Krishnamurti,1987:16)

In many senses this puts a great deal of responsibility on to the individual - much more than modern society usually accredits to the population. To instigate political change, one's own affairs are not only the starting point but an end in themselves. Society is what each of us perpetuates in our everyday existence, hence there is no dividing line between personal change and communal change. Real change in society will only be affected by the inner psychological transformation of the individual. Otherwise society will still incorporate the same problems, such as static repetitive structures, if there is only a surface change, not a deeper more fundamental shift. Without a transformation of the individual, change merely in the outer structures will have no significance. Society will continue to decay if modifications are achieved only through such mechanisms as legislation or macro-structures, without the corresponding inward alteration. It is this inward change, a change in the mind of the individual, that is the only way society can be improved. Otherwise external measures are simply like a cosmetic covering over a rotten core:

> Outward action, when accomplished, is over, is static; if the relationship between individuals, which is society, is not the outcome of inward revolution, then the social structure, being static, absorbs the individual and therefore makes him equally static, repetitive. (Krishnamurti, 1987:18)

In order to make this inward transition the essential prerequisite is self-knowledge, one must first know oneself to begin this process of change. To be is to be related, no one can live in isolation, so the problem can be solved by formulating the right relationships. Where there are bad relationships, such relationships will bring about conflict. Conversely, if we transform our relationships it will be like a wave extending outward to all facets of society:

> Thus the transformation of the world is brought about by the transformation of oneself, because the self is the product and a part of the total process of human existence. To transform oneself, self-knowledge is essential; without knowing what you are, there is no basis for right thought, and without knowing yourself there cannot be transformation. (Krishnamurti, 1987:23)

This self-knowledge, self-understanding, is one of the major tenets in Krishnamurti's thought. For him it is the beginning of all intellectual processes; if one cannot understand one's own being, then Krishnamurti argues, it is impossible to understand anything else. This self-knowledge is the first step in knowledge accumulation; to forgo this stage will result in a perpetual misunderstanding, as information acquired without this basis will always be superficial. It is through such self-knowledge that real change/revolution in society can occur and this must be located at an individual psychological level for the change to be far-reaching. For the individual to understand what s/he really is will be the beginning of virtue. Virtue will give the individual freedom, freedom from what the individual is not. When the individual is not trying to be something, not striving for an abstract ideal, then s/he can have the freedom to be who s/he is. For the individual to try to become something that s/he is not is a form of postponement, a covering up what is, with what s/he wants to be. "Virtue is not the becoming of what is not; virtue is the understanding of what *is* and therefore freedom from what *is*."(Krishnamurti, 1987:24)

To achieve this self-knowledge and therefore an understanding of what *is*, can be a complex process within a Western intellectual framework. For Krishnamurti, however, it is a process of simple contemplation of what is around us. Krishnamurti's formulation of reality is a world in constant flux and perpetual movement. In order to understand the *actual*, this constantly changing reality, a very alert and swift mind is required to fully appreciate the fast moving complexities of life. This process of understanding reality is one of passively watching what is going on from moment to moment. This is undertaken by the individual examining what they are actually doing, what it is they are, not what they want to be: "It is not the ideal, because the ideal is fictitious, but it is actually what you are doing, thinking and feeling from moment to moment." (Krishnamurti,1987:24)

This passivity of knowledge acquisition illustrates one of the crucial aspects of Krishnamurti's thought; the attempt to eliminate divisive practices caused by the analysing mind. Krishnamurti argues that one of the main reasons why people are incapable of self-knowledge is because the brain works in such well worn grooves, that it never catches anything new. The mind always tries to put things in categories, form definitions and compare, and once these mechanisms are in operation nothing new can be detected. The mind will slip into its normal thought patterns and negate change. To understand what *is* requires a state of mind in which there is no identification or condemnation and a state of alertness with passive contemplation.

Such intellectual mechanisms of analysis enable a process of separation to take place, a separation between the individual and society. The individual can view society in an abstract framework and therefore see it as of no direct concern to them, or only of concern in a once removed sense. This creates division between the two entities. The solution to this division created by abstract thought is to:

> find out how to look so that one sees all the things that are happening, outside or inside oneself, as a unitary process, as a total movement. Either one looks at the world from a particular point of view - taking a stand verbally, ideological, committed to a particular action and therefore isolated from the rest - or one looks at this whole phenomenon as a living, moving process, a total movement of which one is a part and from which one is not divided. (Krishnamurti,1986:15)

This method of abstract thought is prevalent in all cultures and Krishnamurti highlights this as the essential cause of division and separation in the world. When ideological structures or thought patterns are used, then a predetermined stand has been taken long before the data is actually considered and *a priori* categories already formed. This deductive methodology colours the proceedings and makes it impossible to look at the whole process - and this will lead to fragmentation between what *is* (which is constantly changing) and what you perceive (which is conceptualized as immutable). [3] "Explanations blind you, they prevent you from actually seeing "what is"." (Krishnamurti,1986:16)

In place of this dualistic methodology Krishnamurti offers the alternative of a mind freed from preconception, passively watching experiences from moment to moment. This requires an alert and disciplined thought process. Discipline in this context means neither suppression and control nor an adjustment to a pattern or an ideology; it is simply a mind that sees "what *is*". An explanation of how discipline, in its traditional context, forms dualistic categories illustrates Krishnamurti's analysis of these dividing practices. In the ordinary sense to discipline oneself implies there is an entity that is disciplining itself according to something. This creates a dualistic process. On the one hand there is the person who wants to do the thing and on the other the thing s/he actually does. These two competing processes give rise to a state of conflict.

> There is a dualistic process: I say to myself, "I must get up early in the morning and not be lazy", or "I must not be angry". That involves a dualistic process. There is the one who with his will tries to control what he should do, as opposed to what he actually does. (Krishnamurti,1986:23)

This dualistic process results from a denial of the actual situation, that is, the person tries to project what they want to happen on to what *is*, creating two versions of reality. This form of living in an ideal and projected future is exacerbated by a modern consumer society that takes this desire to change and channels it into the desire to buy. People come to believe that by exercising a choice over certain products they can effect the change in themselves they wish for. It is the desire for change that results in the formulation of a projected future, producing a never ending process. By living in such a projected future these desires can never be met; it is a jam yesterday, jam tomorrow, never jam today scenario. These changes will never be effected, a perpetual state of conflict is initiated in which there is always a gap between what one is and what one wants.

The conflict is between what one wants to be and what one *is*: "We are slaves to the verb "to be", which implies: "I will be somebody sometime in the future"."(Krishnamurti,1986:25) This becoming process is, to Krishnamurti's mind, what prevents us from really knowing what we are: if we are always building our plans on some uncertain future state, we will never be confronted with what *is*. Thus: "Self-improvement is the very antithesis of freedom and learning." (Krishnamurti,1986:25) Krishnamurti attempts to liberate us from all systems that prevent freedom and synthesis. All predetermined *a priori* categories create division and impede our ability to fully comprehend reality. "Analysis implies division. There is the analyser and that which is to be analysed. Whether you analyse yourself, or it is done by a specialist, there is division, therefore there is already the beginning of conflict."

(Krishnamurti,1986:32) To Krishnamurti such analysis always results in imposed value judgements. Once the process of comparing and weighing up is started, evaluation is never far behind. This creates further conflict, as the arguments over what is good or bad and so on will form the basis of theory, not the appreciation of reality.

Krishnamurti's formulation of the subject is one that exists not in opposition to, or different from society, but as one part of the greater whole. Society is the relationships that we form with one another. Thus, the individual and society are not two distinct and separate entities, Krishnamurti's subject is society as well, the terms are merged together and both lose their independent meaning. The very construction of the polarity between the individual and society is at issue for Krishnamurti. He criticises the rationalizing abstract thought processes that enable the subject to be divided off from essential components of itself. Further, Krishnamurti argues for the elimination of these barriers and divisions by a rejection of these set abstract thought patterns, that create these barriers in the first instance. There should be greater adherence to "what *is*". This does not presuppose an inviolate reality, but rather Krishnamurti conceives reality to be in a state of flux. Thus, reality has a kaleidoscopic formulation, for which we need an agile mind to comprehend all of these constantly changing circumstances. Another difficulty created by these abstract thought processess is the creation of what can be perceived to be isolated problems, the relational properties of dilemmas masked by an abstract methodology. This methodology leads to inadequate solutions and further division, as divisive practices are built on divisive practices, creating finer and more complex dichotomies, removing the individual further from what *is* and reducing his/her ability to comprehend it. In this way Krishnamurti attempts to overcome the isolation of this individual, an individual created by abstract thought, and formulate a dynamic and reciprocal relationship between the individual and society.

This analysis would be compatible with the humanist tradition because it still recognizes the individual as the site of change and agency, but resists the dichotomizing implications of humanism by a refusal to postulate the individual and society as separate entities. Society is no longer viewed as a distinct entity (whatever ontological status this entity might be said to possess), it is seen as a purely relational construct. This analysis differs from individualism in that it conceptualizes an important and fundamental relationship between individuals - a relationship without which they would not be individuals in the sense by which we understand the term. In this way, different types of relationship will form different types of individuals. A cautionary point has to be raised here, it is hardly accurate to contend that this is Krishnamurti's solution to the individual-society dichotomy, as the problematic has not been constructed in exactly the same way in Indian thought. [4] This dichotomy is one bequeathed by Western epistemological traditions and it is to an author who explicitly engages with these traditions that I will now turn. Michel Foucault puts forward another reconstruction of the subject and seeks to locate it within the mechanisms of discursive practice.

## Foucault and the Subject

The Foucaultian notion of subject is one of the most far-reaching critiques of traditional theories of individuality given in recent philosophy. Foucault illustrates the problematics and historicity of the subject by showing how the very notion of such a subject is constructed. For Foucault the problem is not one of how a certain subject is formulated, but that there is an entity such as the subject, however it is constituted, in the first place. A central aim of his work is to displace all notions of the subject, creating a theory where the subject does not have to rule supreme, and wider objects of study are capable of being placed at the centre of analysis, in the position the subject previously occupied. Hence, under Foucault's system, the individual does not have to occupy a central place in theorizing - any facet of social organization can be placed in this role.

There are two essential points in Foucault's conception of the subject: first, it is a product of the particular disciplinary practices and rationalizing discourses in which it is constructed - the context in which the subject is placed. This idea has been fairly common in modern philosophy and there are many theories concerned with the social construction of individuality (some mentioned above). With these accounts, the effect of a person's cultural environment on their subsequent characteristics has become a well known dictum. Foucault's account of social construction is made more interesting by his theory of discourses, which gives an elucidation of how the subject is actually produced by its environment. The second point is that Foucault problematizes the very idea of having an individual subject in any form, it is this element in his theory that provides a devastating critique of the subject as formulated by individualism.

Foucault's work looks at how humanity has been moulded into various subject types, for instance the way people become subjects of sexuality, and he concentrates on this process of formulation. The crucial issue is the notion that people can be divided off and delineated into subjects of a specific discourse. The exposition of what produces the characteristics of the subject, namely the constraints, normalizing processes or power operations a person will be subjected to, is a secondary consideration in Foucault's work. Under this account it is not what happens to the subject after it is conceived, but the very fact it is conceived in any form that is the basis of his intensive critique of the individual subject. This has implications for the analysis considered in the previous chapter,

this historical contextualization needed to be something more than the simple relativisation of the phenomenological subject. I don't believe the problem can be solved by historicising the subject as posited by the phenomenologists, fabricating a subject that evolves through the course of history. One has to dispense with the constituent subject, to get rid of the subject itself, that is to say, to arrive at an analysis which can account for the constitution of the subject within a historical framework. (Foucault,1980:117)

Therein lies the value of Foucault's analysis: he attempts to formulate a world where the subject would not always have to take precedence or even exist.

It is in this way that Foucault strikes at the very heart of humanism, arguing that humanism's subject matter (the person) is a specifically constructed entity that operates within a certain time and place, not an abstract predetermined being. Therefore, this being is a product of its time and what the humanist would see as humanity (formulated as an abstract entity) is in fact a culturally conditioned subjectivity. The subject that individualism takes as the area of concern, through its construction within society, has become imbued with the characteristics of a Western masculine elite and these characteristics have been given the status of universal truths. By illustrating how the subject is created by discourses specific to its context, he aims to show that these universal claims about human nature are unjustified and historically incorrect.

In order to give a detailed account of this Foucaultian subject it is useful to consider both his methodology and his formulation of power relations, as these form important elements in his theorizing. In Foucault's view, subjects are created to fit into unitary and normalizing structures and this leads directly to a theory of the subject that demands a monolithic morality. By creating several uniform theories of the subject out of humanity's diverse and contradictory nature, power and discipline are able to operate more persuasively. The power structures that are created require uniform demands from each individual and, once these individuals have been conditioned into regarding themselves as certain types of subject, they can aspire to conform to these demands. The fact that many people cannot and do not conform is beside the point; the issue here is that in certain respects we all try and those who truly cannot are pathologized. The relationship between truth and power is an important aspect of Foucault's work, but his predominate concern is with the formulation of the subject. In Foucault's words:

> I would like to say, first of all, what has been the goal of my work in the last twenty years. It has not been to analyze the phenomena of power, nor to elaborate the foundations of such an analysis. My objective, instead, has been to create a history of the different modes by which, in our culture, human beings are made subjects. (Foucault,1982:208)

To explain this process of subject formulation, Foucault considers power and its structures, inverting many traditional notions of how power operates within society. When he analyses the system of right, the domain of law, Foucault argues that this should be considered, "not in terms of a legitimacy to be established but in terms of the methods of subjugation that it instigates." (Foucault,1980:96) In this way Foucault transposes conventional discussions of right, centering upon sovereignty and obedience, with the problem of dominance and subjugation. The methodological precautions pertaining to these considerations are outlined in a lecture given in 1976 (Foucault,1980), and an account of these provides an excellent insight into Foucault's theory of the subject, there are five methodological precautions, "that seemed requisite to its pursuit."(Foucault,1980:96)

First, the analysis should be concerned neither with power in its regulated legitimate forms, nor at its central location, but should concentrate on power operating at its local source, at its extremities. To illustrate this local functioning of power, Foucault uses the example of punishment. Rather than looking at the right of punishment in terms of its basis in sovereignty and democratic rights, Foucault considers the ways punishment is embodied in local and material institutions - at its point of exercise and application, "one should try to locate power at the extreme points of its exercise, where it is always less legal in character."(Foucault,1980:97) In this way, the analysis will be concerned with prisons, policemen and the actual forms of punishment an individual will be subjected to, not an abstract philosophical discourse on theories of retribution or confinement. In his book *Discipline and Punish: The birth of the prison*, Foucault provides an illustration of this methodology, in his examination of mechanisms of control. He focuses on the functionings of power at its extremities by considering the prisons, schools and modes of torture themselves and their specific methods of discipline.

Second, power cannot be looked at from an internal point of view, at the level of conscious intention or decision. This would take the form of asking such questions as, "who then has the power and what has he in mind?" Within Foucault's perspective these are complex and unanswerable questions and do not constitute profitable areas of study. To effectively examine power, questions should be aimed at the level where it is in direct and immediate relationship with its object, its field of application, where power produces effects and intersects with the subject. Hence, questions should be aimed at how things work at the level of on-going subjugation:

> In other words, rather than ask how the sovereign appears to us in his lofty isolation, we should try to discover how it is that subjects are gradually, progressively, really and materially constructed through a multiplicity of organisms, forces, energies, materials, desires, thoughts, etc. We should try to grasp subjection in its material instance as a constitution of subjects...rather than worry about the problem of the central spirit, I believe we must attempt to

study the myriad of bodies which are constituted as peripheral *subjects* as a result of the effects of power. (Foucault,1980:97-98)

This methodology is contrasted with that of Hobbes' *Leviathan*, in which, Foucault argues, Hobbes is attempting to reduce the complexity of many individual wills to, "a single will - or rather, the constitution of a unitary, singular body animated by the spirit of sovereignty - from particular wills of a multiplicity of individuals." (Foucault, 1980:97)

The third methodological precaution is that power should not be conceived as one individual's domination over another (this is the internal view). Rather, power should be seen as something that is never solely in one person's hands; it is employed more through the mechanisms of net-like organizations than located in one area. This perpetuation of power by these net-like organizations does not imply that it is evenly distributed, it is not democratically diffused. Under this account all individuals will be experiencing the power exercised by others while at the same time exercising power over others themselves, although some will be exercising more than others. The individual is not the sole area where power is produced and carried out; power operates predominantly by the very construction of certain bodies and discourses which influence the formulation of individual characteristics. In this way, individuals are vehicles of power, not its point of application:

> The individual is not to be conceived as a sort of elementary, nucleus, a primitive atom, a multiple and inert material on which power comes to fasten or against which it happens to strike, and in so doing subdues or crushes individuals. In fact, it is already one of the prime effects of power that certain bodies, certain gestures, certain discourses, certain desires, come to be identified and constituted as individuals. The individual, that is, is not the *vis-a-vis* of power; it is, I believe, one of its prime effects. The individual is an effect of power, and at the same time, or precisely to the extent to which it is that effect, it is the element of its articulation. The individual which power has constituted is at the same time its vehicle. (Foucault,1980:98)

This gives a much broader application of theories of power and enables areas not covered by conventional definitions of power to be brought under analysis and put into the context of the functionings of power relations.

The fourth methodological precaution leads directly from the former: the analysis should be ascending, beginning at the bottom extremities of power application. In order to study power effectively, the analysis should not be concentrated at the central location of power, the government, the state apparatus and so forth. This type of power analysis begins at the centre and follows its application outward to the base of society, analysing how it permeates down to molecular elements.

In Foucault's view the analysis must be an ascending one, starting from the most minute mechanisms,

> which each have own history, their own trajectory, their own techniques and tactics, and then see how these mechanisms of power have been - and continue to be - invested, colonised, utilised, involuted, transformed, displaced, extended etc., by ever more general mechanisms and by forms of global domination. (Foucault,1980:99)

Foucault's consideration of madness illustrates how an ascending explanation of power would explain phenomenon.

A traditional descending form of analysis would look at the domination of the bourgeois class and from this deduce the effects such a domination had on the treatment of those perceived to be unstable - the internment of the insane for example. An ascending analysis, in contrast, would not look at an amalgamated term such as the "bourgeoisie", as this would provide only a "glib" and vague analysis. What should be considered are the basic units of society - the family, doctors, parents, etc. A greater depth of understanding can be produced by examining these "real agents" than by considering a general formula of the bourgeoisie, which in practice can never be accurately analysed and is simply a generalization designed for intellectual convenience. These basic units of power mechanisms operate in specific incidents at specific times, however, the central issue for Foucault is the transformation of these operations into economically and politically useful tools. By following this analysis through, it can be seen that the bourgeoisie did not particularly need the internment of the insane (as one system can tolerate opposite practices) but it did need the techniques and procedures of the repressive practices that this internment portrayed. These micro-mechanisms of power, at that time, represented the interests of the bourgeoisie, resulting in their colonization by global structures and state systems:

> The bourgeoisie could not care less about the delinquents, about their punishment and rehabilitation, which economically have little importance, but it is concerned about the complex of mechanisms with which delinquency is controlled, pursued, punished, and reformed etc. (Foucault,1980:102)

Hence, interest is not in the manifestation of deviance itself, but the power mechanisms that were used to suppress it. By using this ascending analysis it is possible to perceive the localized applications of power and thus understand more fully the way in which, "these mechanisms come to be effectively incorporated into the social whole." (Foucault,1980:101)

The final methodological precaution is the recognition that the major mechanisms of power are accompanied by certain practices, like education, democracy and the monarchy, for instance. These practices have traditionally been seen as ideological structures, but Foucault argues that these are not ideologies in the usual sense of the term. They are, at the same time, both much more and much less than that. Foucault sees these practices as the production of effective instruments for the formation of knowledge. Power will evolve and will put into circulation apparatuses of knowledge and these apparatuses cannot be considered as ideological constructs. The reason they cannot be considered as ideologies is because these apparatuses of knowledge are the producers of the effective instruments for the very formulation and accumulation of knowledge, namely the criteria by which all knowledge is judged and evaluated. In this way power structures will create a knowledge that legitimizes it, a knowledge that is produced by and provides justification for structures and discourses. "All this means that power, when it is exercised through these subtle mechanisms, cannot but evolve, organise and put into circulation a knowledge, or rather apparatuses of knowledge, which are not ideological constructs." (Foucault,1980:102)

By outlining these methodological precautions Foucault's version of how the subject is formed is further elucidated. Power is dethroned; no longer is it a tool only a few people in society wield, a tool controlling the more public side of our life, state institutions for instance. Under Foucault's analysis it is a more persuasive dominating influence extending into every facet of our lives. The power/knowledge structures are present at local and personal levels and consequently have immediate and practical effects.

As this analysis of power employs a methodology that is an ascending appraisal, starting from the smallest mechanisms and following them upwards to their more global manifestations, with this methodology certain barriers are overcome or problematized. The public/private split between the various domains of people's lives is an example of the elimination of a previously conceived dichotomy. By virtue of the way Foucault conceives power exerting a controlling influence over us, it does not cease to operate when the doors are closed on the outside world. Previous notions of power would conceive its influence as functioning to a greater extent in the outside world, by mechanisms such as the police force, the state, the army, etc. [5] As long as one does not break the law laid down by the legislature, in the privacy of the home one can do as one chooses. [6]

Under this analysis people are deemed to be essentially free from outside influence once they retreat into their private domains. Although men and women have had very different experiences relating to this dichotomy, [7] the home has always been seen as the area where true natural family values can flourish. Foucault's formulation of power erodes this distinction between different spheres of power influence and conceptualizes the effects power/knowledge will have on them. Power is no longer solely exerted in the outside world, the public domain - it is just as forcibly present in the private realm. Areas hitherto thought as unconnected to power structures, such as sexuality and madness, are now seen as direct results of these power structures.

This reappraisal of how power operates breaks down aspects of the public/private split. Power is no longer conceived as coming solely from above, because individuals are the vehicles of power, not simply the point of application. This enables power to extend into areas not previously thought to be subject to power relations, widening the definition of power and drawing a much greater area of human experience into the debate. The very categories people place themselves in, in relation to others, such as normal, deviant, insane and disturbed, are, according to Foucault, products and applications of the power/knowledge structure. This all-pervasive concept of power operation floods over conventional barriers, destroying in its wake domains previously thought to be above and beyond this form of external control.

I now want to consider the specific way the subject is constituted under Foucault's analysis, in order to provide a clearer picture of this theory of subjectivity. Foucault highlights certain modes of objectification which transform human beings into the distinct entities he calls subjects, and examines the history of these different modes within our culture. Foucault draws attention to three main modes of objectification, the first is the modes of inquiry which give themselves the status of sciences. These disciplines objectify people by creating a certain model of what it is to be a person that will fit into their field of research - the objectification of the speaking subject in philology and linguistics, the objectification of the productive subject in economics, and the objectification of just being alive that is produced by natural history and biology, for instance. These sciences create an idea of humanity, a preconceived subject that becomes a tool to characterize people and analyses them in a static formulation - humans as objectified subjects rather than diverse and disparate individuals.

The second mode of objectification is what Foucault calls the "dividing practices". The subjects are divided from themselves or others and this very process objectifies them. These dividing practices are mechanisms such as the mad versus the insane, the sick and the healthy, the criminals and law-abiding citizens. People become able to put themselves in categories that are defined in opposition to others, "I am this but s/he is that". Identity is thus drawn in contrast to other categories, these categories forming yard-sticks to compare and judge different types of humanity.

The final mode is the way humans turn themselves into subjects. As an example of this Foucault concentrates of sexuality, [8] an area where people have learnt to recognize themselves as subjects of an historically constituted sexuality. The very categories of sexuality are defined and produced by discursive discourses and people locate themselves within them without realizing the specificity of their formulation. When these modes of objectification are viewed in the context of Foucault's methodological precautions, it becomes clear to see how these seemingly abstract formulations can have practical results.

Throughout his work Foucault gives detailed historical evidence and practical examples to shore up his claims. Unfortunately space does not allow the detailed consideration of these illustrations, just an elucidation of the theoretical underpinnings.

The area of sexuality provides a useful summary of how Foucault conceives these mechanisms of objectification taking effect. Power has two facets (which he uses as a basis for his theorizing): the repressive hypothesis and bio-power. The former is something Foucault fervently disagrees with - that truth can be seen to be in contrast to power structures and its application will result in social justice. This view presupposes that power abuse is based on faulty perceptions of a certain reality, a notion contrary to Foucault's system of constructed realities. For Foucault truth and power are intimately intertwined and do not stand in contradiction to each other. [9] To provide an alternative to this repressive hypothesis Foucault interprets the relationship between sex, truth, power, the body and the individual, as a network he calls bio-power, and this synthesis will be considered in further detail. According to Dreyfus and Rabinow's (1982) elucidation of Foucault's work, bio-power coalesced around two poles at the beginning of the classical age. They remained separated until the nineteenth century, when they converged to form the technologies of power recognizable today.

The first pole was the characterization of the human species into specific structures by scientific discourse. Scientific concepts became the object of political contention, replacing judicial concepts as the main focus. Elements in the categorizing of the human species such as population and birth-control now became political tools, upon which further functionings of power could operate. Sex and reproduction had political ramifications and were areas to be controlled, becoming the business of the politician. The second pole of bio-power saw the body not as a means of reproduction, but as an object to be manipulated. The aim of these disciplinary powers was to create a human being who could be treated as a docile body; not only this, the subject also had to fulfil a useful function. When examining the means of correct training in *Discipline and Punish*, Foucault considers the specific applications of these disciplinary powers,

> discipline brought with it a specific way of punishing that was not only a small-scale model of the court. What is specific to the disciplinary penalty is non-observance, that which does not measure up to the rule, that departs from it. The whole indefinite domain of non-conforming is punishable: the soldier commits an "offence" whenever he does not reach the level required; a pupil's "offence" is not only a minor infraction, but also an inability to carry out his tasks. (Foucault,1991:178-179)

Discipline such as this was exerted in many areas not only the barracks, prisons and hospitals. In this way politics became bio-politics. As Foucault states:

> from the idea that the state has its own nature and its own finality, to the idea that man is the true object of the state's power, as far as he produces a surplus strength, as far as he is a living, working, speaking being, as far as he constitutes a society, and as far as he belongs to a population in an environment, we can see the increasing intervention of the state in the life of the individual. The importance of life for these problems of political power increases; a kind of animalization of man through the most sophisticated political techniques results. Both the development of the possibilities of the human and social sciences, and the simultaneous possibility of protecting life and of the holocaust make their historical appearance. (Quoted in Dreyfus & Rabinow, 1982:138)

The state adopted a new focus. When previously it had been concerned with men as subjects with rights and duties, it was now interested in men's commonplace lives, as the formal components of the state. Administrators needed exact knowledge about their populace and similar information about other countries. This was an essential element in the survival of the nation, as the power of the state relied on comparisons with others to ensure they would not be outstripped, (a practical elucidation of the Machiavellian fear that one way to lose liberty would be if the populace was conquered by another state). The welfare of the populations was not a moral endeavour but one of ensuring the continued strength of the state. The life-cycles of the populace were now a political issue and the structure of populations crucial to the power of the state. As Dreyfus and Rabinow point out:

> Human needs were no longer conceived of as ends in themselves or as subjects of a philosophic discourse which sought to discover their essential nature. They were now seen instrumentally and empirically, as the means for the increase of the state's power. Foucault thus demonstrates the relationship between the new administrative concept of human welfare and the growth of bio-power. (Dreyfus and Rabinow, 1982:139-140)

Through the mechanism of sexuality bio-power extended its influence into every facet of human life. Sexuality was now a tool to exert authoritative control over the populace by bringing together elements such as the body, knowledge, discourses and power. The expanding role of the modern state and the administrative apparatus set up to carry out these increasing mechanisms of control, were very concerned with the structure of the population, which was now regarded in the same light as a resource. All facets of individual lives were important in so far as they related to these political concerns. One of the main functions of the individual was

111

to defend and aid the state and if social welfare produced fitter and healthier individuals more able to pursue this end, then it should be instigated. Thus, the two poles of bio-power became amalgamated in the concern over sexual behaviour that dominated the nineteenth century.

> Sexuality must not be described as a stubborn drive, by nature alien and of necessity disobedient to a power which exhausts itself trying to subdue it and often fails to control it entirely. It appears rather as an especially dense transfer point for relations of power: between men and women, young people and old people, parents and offspring, teachers and students, priests and laity, an administration and a population. Sexuality is not the most intractable element in power relations, but rather one of those endowed with the greatest intrumentality: useful for the greatest number of manoeuvres and capable of serving as a point of support, as a linchpin, for the most varied strategies. (Foucault, 1990:103)

The consolidation of bio-power illustrates how elements usually considered outside the realm of the influence of state power are drawn into the forum and previously unconsidered areas of human nature are seen as cultural constraints.

This outline of Foucault's methodology and power definitions illustrates the framework out of which Foucault's subject emerges. He needs this formulation of the subject so that it can be constructed by the mass of discursive practices to become a subject of the multitudinous discourses, for instance a subject of sexuality or a subject of science. This subject exists in so far as it is located in the discourses that create it, this very construction is an operation of power through its net-like mechanisms.

This is clearly a brief overview of Foucault's theory of subjectivity rather than an all encompassing study and the elements that have been highlighted are those that pertain to the general argument of the book. In order to investigate Foucault's formulation of subjectivity in greater depth, I shall evaluate the impact of the critiques that have been levied against his theorizations.

## Criticisms of Foucault

Foucault's radical reformulation of the subject has given rise to many criticisms, the most pertinent of which will be considered, as far as they relate to the task inhand. Foucault is often charged with holding a cultural relativist position in an extreme form. This states that there is nothing essential or static in humanity, nor is there anything static or underlying about values or truth criteria. The only judge of acceptability is the community in which ideas are located; there is no ahistorical rationality to appeal to for validation. Politically this conclusion is repugnant to many theorists on the grounds that people could be particularly susceptible to forms of manipulation if their natures and values were so volatile. Foucault's analysis strikes further into the culturally conditioned realm than most, so consequently he is seen as advancing theories with dangerous practical ramifications. On a philosophical level this cultural relativism can cause problems for the role the observer plays in inquiry. If, under Foucault's analysis, we are so formulated by discursive practices to the extent that even our sexuality is subjugated, how can we pull this apart and analyse it? Where is our point of reference? It is the Archimedian problem of moving the earth from a position inside the earth itself.

The problem to which such an approach can lead is articulated by P L Brown:

> Foucault, as a sane participant in Western civilization joining and furthering the tradition of rational letters, can no more speak the language of discontinuity than he can the language (or silence) of madness; he can only speak *of* them from his own "centre" of Western philosophic rationalism. (Brown, 1975:158)

The inability to stand fully outside the structures and definitions could be seen as a problem for Foucault's analysis. If Foucault's formulation of the subject is an adequate one, then he, as a subject himself, would be constructed in the same way, locked in certain discourses and unable to see beyond them.

Foucault does not give an explicit answer to the question of where he places himself in his descriptive framework. As Dreyfus and Rabinow point out, by his archaeological method he can achieve a partial distance from the terms of description he employs - but not a total one. Foucault criticizes the structures that inject rationality into what he sees as the discontinuous events of history - this is what Foucault calls the "problem of reason". "I think that we must limit the sense of the word "rationalization" to an instrumental and relative use...and to see how forms of rationalizations become embodied in practices, or systems of practices." (Quoted in Dreyfus & Rabinow, 1982:133)

If Foucault's analysis is taken as an historical formulation rather than a metaphysical one then the problem, of the position of the speaker's location created by Foucault's relativism can to a certain extent be circumvented. Under this account Foucault will face an historical problem, not an insurmountable clash of metaphysical levels. By constructing the problem in this way, it is now possible to provide a basis for the theorizing, since the prerequisite that one had to be in some way "outside" these processes of rationalization can be seen as an historical, not a metaphysical, imperative. This needs to be explained; a metaphysical prerequisite would make it impossible to remove oneself and step "outside" the discursive practices. By the very nature of the rationalizing processes Foucault sets up, he would be as much a product of these discursive practices as the structures he criticizes. This prerequisite would make it difficult for Foucault to argue for the historical specificity of the subject, for he could not tell what was a historical formulation versus a natural one. Consequently, it would be a critique from within, one historically constructed entity to another, both equally blinded by their formulation.

Foucault overcomes this problem by not attacking reason itself, but by attacking instead the way in which a form of historic rationality has functioned, thus providing a solid base on which to build his theorizing. He can criticize this specific form of rationality by using the tool of reason and therefore avoid the problems that relativism creates. [10] Equipped with his methods of archaeology and genealogy he attempts a concrete analysis of his chosen themes: the relationships between truth and power and the practical effects these incur. This is illustrated by examining how Foucault envisages this analysis progressing:

> I would like to suggest another way to go further towards a new economy of power relations, a way which is more empirical, more directly related to our present situation, and which implies more relations between theory and practice. It consists of taking the forms of resistance against different forms of power as a starting point. To use another metaphor, it consists of using this resistance as a chemical catalyst so as to bring to light power relations, locate their position, find out their point of application and the methods used. Rather than analyzing power from the point of view of its internal rationality, it consists of analyzing power relations through the antagonisms of strategies. (Foucault, 1982:210-211)

In the context of an historical framework, the subject will be constructed by a web of discourses, themselves a product of their historical setting. These constructs can be analyzed by the tools of reason, but still retain their status in opposition to *a priori* truths - contingent truths (or subjects) can still be participants in inquiry. Dreyfus and Rabinow make the point:

> As we argue throughout this book, Foucault's method of interpretive analytics was constructed as a powerful and necessary tool to avoid the dilemma of value-freedom which haunted Weber or the temptation of irrationalism and despair (or recourse to art) which was never far from the Frankfurt thinkers. Foucault is eminently reasonable; this has lead him to centre his work on the practical operation of "the truth" in modern regimes of power. (Dreyfus & Rabinow, 1982:133)

Due to the use of an historical framework, Foucault can ground himself in the stability of reason and side-step the relativist's dilemma.

The question of the validity of Foucault's historical analysis is often raised when assessing his work. The issue has been considered above in Chapter Three but an additional point has to be made: a defender of Foucault must not fall into the trap of rescuing his work from relativism by claiming its historical and reasoned basis is valid and countering the historians who attack his thesis on the grounds that it is built on a different metaphysical basis from the one that underpins conventional history. In order for this analysis to stand, Foucault's work must be subject to the same criticisms other historians face. This project is complicated by the nature of his methodology which approaches the material from a radically different perspective. In this way both the process and the conclusions Foucault's history reaches distance him from a traditional historical approach and the way such approaches are criticized. Nevertheless, although it is complicated to assimilate Foucault into the discipline of history, he is still susceptible to criticisms directed at his accuracy in recounting events and data. Foucault is concerned with the rationalizations behind historical facts and the interpretive meaning, the contention that they happened at all is not one he takes issue with.

These problems of relativism appear to come to a head when considering Foucault's formulation of the subject. In his view every concept that is used to talk about humanity is constructed by discursive practices and the very idea of having a subject at all is similarly formed. This results in we ourselves forming part of that process and making us unable to stand apart, locked in discursive practices. To an extent this can be countered by the historical approach outlined above which is that as long as these formulations are seen as specifically constructed entities then the theory has done its job. Even though we are constructed this does not imply we are unable to analyse other constructed subjects. With Foucault's elimination of conventional value criteria, we do not have to see one subject construction as truer and therefore "better" than another, however we can still recognize difference without needing to infer the possession of an implicit status.

Another problem with Foucault's analysis is that it can be argued that he never circumvents the problem of the homunculus, namely at what point in the individual's existence do these discursive practices begin to operate. Nowhere does Foucault explicitly state how this problem is to be overcome. He seems to be saying that these practices, through the extensive net-like operations of power, influence us and form us into subjects from the moment we are born. If these practices are operations of power and distortion, which differ through each historical age, then this could imply a static, underlying notion of human nature, something concrete to distort, upon which these mechanisms of power operate. In this way, there would still remain a problem of the homunculus, an already existent entity with, presumably, some characteristics or at least the potentiality for certain characteristics. However, this charge can be seen as irrelevant to his overall aims. Foucault, unlike other social theorists is not trying to uncover the "true" or correct version of humanity, thus he is not concerned with when these practices begin to operate - or how much is a response to natural faculties. Foucault's theory does not have to admit a pre-given, predetermined entity to be able to criticize power structures or construct ethical systems. It is not a problem for his system that all forms of human nature are in some way conditioned responses and ultimately flexible. The point at issue is the power structures that result from these forms of human nature. If the power structures formulated are not deemed to be oppressive or immoral then that is enough for Foucault, such ethical imperatives do not have to be based on a naturalized theory of human nature. Foucault criticizes totalizing ethical theories and argues that they should not be constructed on some idea of what is natural and hence right for humanity. The concern for Foucault here is one of freedom, something that ethical systems seek to safeguard, not a monolithic freedom, but one that will vary as historical epochs and discursive practices vary, John Rajchman makes the point,

> in taking up the idea of freedom, Foucault sought to rethink it: our freedom would not lie in our essence but in our historically contingent singularity. In this sense, the experience of freedom would not be an experience of an identity or a natural or pregiven state, but, on the contrary, an experience of the fragility of a kind of identification taken for granted. Who we are would not be the image or source of this freedom, but just what is constantly freed or opened to question by it. Thus, it is not in our basic individualities or communities that we are free; it is rather the historical forms of our individual and communal being themselves which must be freed or exposed to the risks of the new and unforeseen transformations. (Rajchman,1991:109-110)

Ethical imperatives have traditionally been based on specific theories of human nature to ascertain what is naturally right for humans and therefore what is good. A theory of completely conditioned human nature is often criticized on the grounds that it would remove any basis for moral theorizing. Foucault's system argues that an ethical system can still be built even on this new conception of the subject. As long as no appeal to ethical imperatives is made on the basis of an abstract human nature but on recognizable constructed forms of the subject and still viewed as ethical, no problem arises. There is no longer any need for the postulation of an abstract human nature; there can be a totally conditioned theory of human nature that does not lead to a schism between morality and power, because for Foucault truth will not guarantee morality. [11]

Foucault's system is a concerted attack against the presupposition of *a priori* categories. He tries to think beyond conventional thought patterns by a process of questioning the basic constructs that are used to order our experiences. Part of his theoretical framework is the analysis, not of a history of progression or continuity but of a history of discontinuity. He sees history as consisting of a series of discontinuous events, only linked together into some form of coherence by a Western rationalizing mind creating the continuities. The structures are imposed on events; it is the *a priori* categories that give this appearance of coherence, history does not possess any form of continuity in itself.

Therefore, his theory of human nature is one that does not attribute any abstract traits to humanity; all is constructed by the discourses in which the subject is enmeshed.

To look more deeply at Foucault's formulation of subjectivity through a focus on his construction of power relations and their political implications, I want to consider one response to Foucault's work, that of a particular school of feminist thought. There has been considerable debate, largely since the 1980s, about the possible interface between feminism and postmodernism. Two broad positions have been taken: those who argue that feminism and postmodernism are natural allies and those who argue that postmodernism is antithetical to the feminist project. [12] It is the latter school of thought that I shall concentrate on, because it raises possible tensions in Foucault's construction of subjectivity and draws attention to the practical affects of postmodernism.

One of the major charges that has been levied at Foucault's theory of subjectivity is his indifference to difference, his failure to consider the specificity of gender. [13] This school of feminist theorists has argued that what is problematic in Foucault's work is the gender blindness of his theory and contends that this blindness eschews strategies of women's liberation. What has been of concern is the possible effect on political action and women's agency. As Hekman states: "Several feminist critiques of the subject focus on the question of agency and argue that feminism must reject the postmodern critique of the subject because it obviates the possibility of agency." (Hekman,1990:80) Postmodernism is thus taken to be quite simply the "death of man" and by implication woman. The notion of an essentialist and foundationalist drive that has characterized previous modernist conceptions of women is rebuked in favour of an ever changing, historically situated subjectivity that eschews attempts to define universal woman.

In response to this, feminists have argued that the abandoning of difference makes any feminist project unfeasible: [14] no longer are we able to speak as a group or a class who might have experienced similar conditions due to the specificity of our gender, we are subdued to speaking only from individual reference points.

There are two interrelated problems with Foucault's perceived indifference to difference that theorists have highlighted: his deconstruction of gender identities removes the possibility of talking as women, since there can be no broad meaning of the term, only localized specificities. Second, it follows that there can be no possibility of agency and therefore no political action within such a system - this would effectively rip the heart out of any active socio-political feminist resistance. These critiques explicitly suggest that erasure of difference could be, "a theory whose time has come for men but not for women." (Nicholson,1990:6) It is argued that although it is a feasible project for men to wish, "to subject [the modernist] legacy to critical scrutiny," (DiStefano,1990:75) women, however, are not yet in that position of assured subject status as men are. As Braidotti states, "one cannot deconstruct a subjectivity one has never been fully granted; one cannot diffuse a sexuality which has historically been defined as dark and mysterious." (Braidotti,1987:237) Women have a different agenda from men and need, at least initially, "to become the subjects of discourse instead of its objects," (Grosz,1990:103) before it is possible to move on to a critique of that subject status. Consequently, for women, the postmodernist project could mean a return, "in updated garb, of the modernist case of the incredible shrinking woman." (DiStefano,1990:77)

On these terms what is needed to readdress the imbalance in the situation of women is the location of the project within gender specificity, as a pivotal point of analysis. Women need to first find that very subjectivity, which has for so long been denied them, before they can benefit from a complete eradication of subjectivity altogether. As Nancy Schor notes: "At the risk of being a wallflower at the carnival of plural sexualities, I would ask: what is it to say that the discourse of sexual indifference/pure difference is not the last ruse of phallocentrism?" (Schor,1989:57)

Rather than providing an exhaustive overview of these critiques, I shall outline Nancy Hartsock's analysis of the relationship between postmodernism and feminism, as her work is representative of these positions and provides an indication of the tenor of the debate.

Hartsock criticises both Foucault's theory of the subject and his methodology, and concentrates on the inadequacy of his formulation of power relations. Foucault's analysis of power, she argues, does not lead to any profound reversals of existing inequalities within society and this is unacceptable for an adequate and useful definition of power. Hartsock summarizes her criticisms:

> First, despite his obvious sympathy for those who are subjugated in various ways, he writes from the perspective of the dominator, "the self-proclaimed majority." Second and related, perhaps in part because power relations are less visible to those who are in a position to dominate others, systematically unequal relations of power ultimately vanish from Foucault's account of power - a strange and ironic charge to make against someone who is attempting to illuminate power relations. (Hartsock,1990:165)

Hartsock's first criticism is not a reiteration of the problem mentioned above: how can Foucault speak the language of discontinuity when he is as locked in the discursive practices as the subject he attempts to deconstruct? Rather, Hartsock criticizes Foucault's idea of power as one that is "with" as opposed to "against" power, that is, his theory of power legitimizes the controlling structures rather than seeking to overthrow them. In this way she argues that Foucault writes from within, from the perspective of the ruling group. He does this in two ways: first, Foucault along with the ruling group perceives other "knowledges" to be illegitimate or, "not allowed to function within official knowledge." (Hartsock,1990:167) This is how Foucault categorizes workers' knowledge for instance, as "counter discourses" or "antisciences", thus failing to appreciate their material and organizational basis. These other "knowledges" cannot be ruled out as nonsystematic as this simply apes conventional methods of excluding alternative discourses.

Second, Foucault stresses resistance to existing power relations rather than a radical transformation and destruction of such relationships, and Hartsock argues this can be seen to be working within existing structures. Intellectuals should not join movements for fundamental change but struggle against the mechanisms of power that turn these movements into instruments of domination. Further, Foucault articulates the undesirable results of going beyond this limited role, in that by adopting these practices of transformation, participation in the existing system is extended. The possible result of such a radical social transformation could have detrimental consequences, which would extend instead of decrease the influence of power structures. Foucault argues that political systems along the lines of the USSR under Stalin could be produced by these transformations.

Thus Hartsock argues that Foucault's system both de-legitimizes alternative discourses and creates no place in the analysis for substantial change. This results in those who have been oppressed within society accepting and remaining in that position.

Hartsock's second criticism that unequal power relations disappear within Foucault's system strikes a blow to his theory of subject construction. This disappearance is produced by his concentration on the heterogeneity and specificity of each situation of power application, resulting in the trivalization of social structures and the privileging of individual points of reference. As was noted above, Foucault perceives that power influences individuals in two ways: an individual will be simultaneously undergoing and exercising power. In other words, the individual will be exerting power over someone else, while being subject to the same process themselves. Under this analysis power cannot be seen as one individual or group having ultimate domination over the other, there is no place for a hierarchy of oppression, all individuals and groups will be subjugated in one way and oppressors in another.

The effects this has on the theorization of gender relations is disastrous in Hartsock's opinion. Foucault's theory only has space for abstract individuals, not women, men or any other particular groups. His elucidation of power operating through net-like mechanisms further evades this issue of domination; such mechanisms seem to incorporate elements of equality and agency, do not provide a theorization of systematic domination of one group over another.

The reason why Foucault's analysis of power fails to strike at the heart of many prevalent operations of power and exploitation within society is, according to Hartsock, in part due to his theory of the subject. She argues that this formulation does not help the theorization of power relations and prejudices important elements within them. In response Hartsock advocates a reinstatement of a specific female subjectivity:

119

rather than getting rid of subjectivity or notions of the subject, as Foucault does, and substituting his notion of the individual as an effect of power relations, we need to engage in the historical, political, and theoretical process of constituting ourselves as subjects as well as objects of history. We need to recognize that we can be the makers of history as well as the objects of those who have made history. (Hartsock,1990:170)

For Hartsock, Foucault's subject cannot take on board the complex factors that have been a facet of women's oppression. Women have traditionally been objects of history and a way forward should not exclude them from attempting to become the subjects of history themselves, in the way men have always been. Foucault's subject is an abstract individual, not located in specific power relations but operating in a web of net-like organizations. This construction of the subject provides no place for a gender-based formulation of subjectivity and results, in Hartsock's view, in a privileging of masculine knowledge and discourse, with a continuation of women as the object of discourse rather than as the subject.

In order to rectify this inadequate construction of the subject, Hartsock argues simultaneously for both a recognition of similarity in developing, "an account of the world which treats our perspectives not as subjugated or disruptive knowledges, but as primary and constitutive of a different world." (Hartsock,1990:171); and a recognition of difference, dissolving the false "we" and seeing the multiplicity of experiences and discourses. Out of these similarities and differences there can be built, "an account of the world as seen from the margins, an account that can expose the falseness of the view from the top." (Hartsock,1990:171) Thus in her analysis there is a need to articulate both commonalities and difference while bearing in mind the problems of constructing totalizing theories.

Hartsock's critique draws out important implications in both Foucault's analysis of power relations and his construction of the subject. His formulation of power seems considerably weaker and less radical than first meets the eye, and Hartsock's recognition of the inability of this theory to construct power differences and unequal relationships is an important criticism of Foucault. The ability of Foucault's subject to adequately overcome the abstract nature of the Cartesian individual is also called into question and highlights a crucial limitation to this construction. Hartsock's critique provides a useful exposition of some of the tensions created and unwelcome conclusions created by this new formulation of the subject as championed by postmodernism.

Although Hartsock's critique makes some important points, I do not think it implies that Foucault's construction of subjectivity should be dismissed out of hand. Foucault's subject goes further towards conceptualizing social influence and provides an illuminating theory of how we become ourselves. Foucault's work is an important foundation upon which to build further constructions of subjectivity.

## Conclusion

Krishnamurti's view of the individual as linked to society in a dynamic relationship and Foucault's constructed subject enmeshed in a web of discourses, provide examples of alternative formulations of the subject. This chapter aimed to show that the concept of the subject provided by individualism and collectivism has alternatives, and is not a necessarily true or universal construction. These first tentative steps in reconstructing the subject have been made to point to ways forward rather than to build a watertight new definition. Nevertheless, these alternative formulations do overcome some of the problems created by an abstract and unitary subject.

These new conceptions of the subject lead to a more elucidating formulation of the relationship between the individual and society - in many ways they actually allow such a relationship to be postulated. The traditional characterization of the subject consisted in a set theory of human nature, a discrete entity, formulated before society even entered into the equation. Society and other environmental factors were thought to act on this pre-given subject. Both Foucault and Krishnamurti's notions of the subject incorporate a much more dynamic form of interaction. For Foucault the very fact there is a subject is due to the operation of external discourses; how we divide ourselves off from one another even in the personal realm is a result of these mechanisms, thus there is no longer an absolute distinction between the individual and society. Not only this, Foucault's analysis goes some way to problematizing the central position of the subject in social theory as mentioned earlier, thus enabling social theory to broaden its scope and consider wider applications of power and new subject matters. In Krishnamurti's view the terms are relational, not distinct entities but a web of relationships operating on the same ontological level, with these relationships working in a reciprocal fashion. This is Krishnamurti's contribution - a theory that can incorporate a total synthesis of the two concepts.

One of the most damaging consequences of the traditional notion of the subject was the universal credence with which it was accepted. It was seen as the sole explanation of human nature: this subject could (under more radical interpretations) be modified by society but essentially humanity had certain, rational, unitary characteristics that had the status of *a priori* truths. The alternative conceptions of the subject attempt to break this universal mould and argue for a much more flexible definition and construction. One of Foucault's major aims was to move away from the idea of totalizing theories. A theory, be it social or psychological, that tries to provide a total explanation of phenomena, is, in Foucault's view, a misguided and impossible project. There will always be anomalies and counter-examples - areas that do not fit into the conceptual schema. One theory of human nature cannot encompass every facet of humanity and the answer is not to construct hundreds of different, conflicting theories, but to create a more flexible analytic structure that can incorporate wider definitions. These wider definitions can then provide a more helpful explanation of humanity not limited to certain set formulas. A deeper understanding of the myriad of factors that influence our views of ourselves and the world can only be a step forward for social theory. Social theory must try not to delineate analysis but broaden it.

# Notes

1. A new definition of the subject is too vast an area to be elucidated in this work, since it involves a reappraisal of many entrenched philosophical positions.

2. See the Conclusion for an overview of the mechanistic world view.

3. Space does not allow for a full critique of this position. See: Chalmers. (1983), *What is this thing called Science?*, Open University Press, Milton Keynes.

4. There is a tradition in anthropological thought that contends that the individual, in the construction that it enjoys in Western cultures, is absent in Indian culture where holism is in precedence. Thus, Krishnamurti would be representing a different tradition that did not have such dichotomizing conceptualizations. See: Dumont, L. (1970), *Homo Hierarchicus: The Caste System and its Implications*, Paladin, London. For a useful critique of the Dumontian view of the construction of the individual in Indian cultures see: Harris, I. (1992), "Individualism and its Indian Context", unpublished paper.

5. See the Introduction for a discussion of liberal notions of what constitutes constraints on freedom.

6. The treatment of domestic violence by the police is an example of the handling the domestic sphere as a private domain and not susceptible to control from outside. ie. the belief a man's home is his castle.

7. See: Elshtain,J.B. (1981), *Public Man, Private Women*, Martin Robertson, Oxford. In this work Elshtain traces the development of the public/private split between spheres of human life: "Distinctions between public and private have been and remain fundamental, not incidental or tangential, ordering principles in all known societies save, perhaps, the most simple." (1981:6) Further, "The public and the private as twin forces help create a moral environment for individuals, singly and in groups; to dictate norms of appropriate or worthy action; to establish barriers to action, particularly in areas such as the taking of human life, regulation of sexual relations, promulgation of familial duties and obligations, and the arena of political responsibility." (1981:5) These ideas are coming to the fore again and this can be shown by the Conservative Government's Back to Basics Campaign in 1993.

8.    See: Foucault,M. (1990), *The History of Sexuality. Vol 1: An Introduction*, Translated Robert Hurley. Penguin, Harmondsworth.

9.    For an exploration of this point concerning truth values, Foucault states:

> The notion of ideology appears to me to be difficult to make use of, for three reasons. The first is that, like it or not, it always stands in virtual opposition to something else that is supposed to count as truth. Now I believe that the problem consists in drawing the line between that in a discourse which falls under the category of scientificity or truth, and that which comes under some other category, but in seeing historically how effects of truth are produced within discourses which in themselves are neither true nor false. (1980:118)

10.   See: Hollis,M. & Lukes,S. (1982), (ed.), *Rationality and Relativism*, Basil Blackwell, Oxford.

11.   There are essentialist conceptions of morality, for example, sociobiologists such as E.O.Wilson, argue that our ethical beliefs are not culturally specific creations but the outcome of an inevitable biology, that is, ethical beliefs are innately determined by our biological make-up. See: Wilson, E,O. (1978), *On Human Nature*, Harvard University Press, Cambridge, Mass. Wilson. (1975), *Sociobiology: The New Synthesis*, Belknap, Cambridge, Mass. Singer,P. (1981), *The Expanding Circle*, Farrar, Strans & Giroux, New York. Singer also considers this biological grounding for ethics and states: "As the sociobiologists say, we are evolved biological organisms and our brains and our emotions reflect the evolutionary adaptations that have enabled us to survive. Our values and ethical systems are the products of our evolved nature. Isn't it then possible that as our knowledge of biology and physiology advance, they should come to reveal ethical premises inherent in our biological nature." (1981:76-77)

12.   For a good introduction to this debate see: McNay, L. (1992), *Foucault and Feminism*, Polity Press, Oxford. Nicholson, L. (ed.), (1990), *Feminism/Postmodernism*, Routledge, London. Hekman, S. (1990), *Gender and Knowledge: Elements of a Postmodern Feminism*, Polity Press, Oxford.

13.   See: Alcoff, L. (1988), "Cultural Feminism Versus Post-Structuralism." in *Signs*, 13 (31). Bordo, S. (1990), "Feminism, Postmodernism and Gender-Scepticism." in Nicholson. Butler, J. (1990), *Gender Trouble*, Routledge, London. DiStefano, C.

(1990), "Dilemmas of Difference: Feminism, Modernity and Postmodernism," in Nicholson. Grosz, E. (1990), "Contemporary Theories of Power and Subjectivity," in Gunew. Soper, K. (1990), *Troubled Pleasures*, Verso, London.

14. There is a current in feminist theory that advocates the reinstatement of essentialist formulations. See: Heath, S. (1978), "Differences," *Screen* 19:3 (Autumn). Jardine, A. (1987), "Men in Feminism: Odor di Komo or Campagnons de Route?" in Jardine and Smith. Spivak, G. (1987), *In Other Worlds: Essays in Cultural Politics*, Methuen, London and New York. For a discussion of this issue see: Fuss, D. (1990), *Essentially Speaking*, Routledge, London.

# Conclusion

This book has been a journey from the abstract to the political, attempting to highlight the practical implications of these abstractions. Within the discipline of philosophy it is often easy to lose sight of the practical aspects of theoretical thought. Consequently, the aim of the book has been to show that abstract theorizing does have implications (albeit not immediate) for practical decision-making and political organization. Along with this, abstract formulations have the potential to bring about certain ends and these ends are not always as divorced from the discussion as people would like to think. The doctrine of individualism, to use the current example, is not a purely abstract and free-floating concept that, once brought to earth and institutionalized, could result in certain social formations; it is an ideological and political concept from the outset and one that arose out of a particular social and political context. The overriding aim of this work has been to illustrate this point.

The discussion began with an appraisal of the traditional debate between the individualists and the collectivists and it was argued that the stalemate between the two positions was due to the implicit theories of human nature upon which both were built. The collectivists were unable to defeat the individualists because they directed their criticisms to the subsidiary arguments of individualism and did not address the fundamental differences in their positions, that is, what each took as characterizing and defining human nature. Individualism is based on an abstract, unitary conception of the subject and this creates theoretical problems for collectivists. If this notion of human nature can be held to be a correct appraisal of reality then this could invalidate the central doctrines of collectivism because the abstract, unitary individual would not fit easily into communal structures, nor indeed have the propensity to do so.

The second chapter expanded this argument by considering how these contrasting perceptions of human nature led to the placing of the

126

individual and society on different sides of an ontological and practical divide, formulating a schism between the individual and society. The chapter then went on to consider attempts to redress this schism, examining areas of social psychology and social theory that had tried to theorize the social construction of the subject. It was argued that the success of these approaches was prejudiced because they continued to formalize the individual and society as two distinct entities, not allowing any rigorous synthesis into their analysis.

Once this unitary abstract subject was highlighted as the major problem in retheorizing the individual-society dichotomy, Chapter Three sought to illustrate the historical specificity of this conception of human nature. Following on from that, the effects such a view of the subject has on academic social psychology was traced and then the practical results of this separation of the individual from society's influences were illustrated by considering the treatment of Afro-Caribbeans within the psychiatric profession.

The final chapter considered alternative formulations of the subject, examining the work of Krishnamurti and Foucault to illustrate how it is possible to think about human nature in radically different ways. A concrete reformulation of the subject was not attempted - the new conceptions were simply presented to illustrate more clearly the failings of the old individualist model. These reformulations of the subject did overcome some of the problems created by the unitary, rational subject: namely, the difficulty in the theorization of the social construction of an individual and the static relationship between the two entities, society and the individual. By problematizing the very contention that the individual and society are two distinct entities, these difficulties are not so much overcome, as they cease to be a matter of theoretical concern.

A further facet of the individualist conception of human nature that was addressed concerned its construction as a culturally and historical specific notion that permeates all branches of knowledge, not simply those concerned directly with human nature such as psychology but abstract disciplines such as science and epistemology as well. With the above points in mind, individualism can be seen in a different light; it is not an abstract, value-free conception of human nature, rather it is a doctrine that has definite practical applications. This is not to say that individualism was constructed with this consciously in mind, it grew out of, and necessitated, post-industrial social relations with each influencing the other in a reciprocal manner. The reciprocal nature of this relationship can partly be theorized by Foucault's notion of discourse, according to which, society consists of many discourses, some competing, some complementary. These discourses influence and inform each other in a multitude of different ways.[1] The predominant discourses, such as scientific objectivity or patriarchy, will be shored up by other less apparent and in some cases contradictory discourses. Under this account, individualism becomes one discourse among many, supporting and supported by other discourses such as the discourse of capitalistic economic relations or the discourse of biological determinism. There is no linear causation at work here; questions such as which discourse came first, or which discourse has the overriding influence are inappropriate within this system of thought.

Traditional formulations of linear causation are inadequate to elucidate the nature of these discourses; they cannot explain how they function or their mechanisms of perpetuation. Consequently, new ways have to be found to delineate these relationships. The idea of many competing discourses cannot fit into an individualistic or even a holistic framework of social explanation. In order to begin a new theory of social causation that can tolerate multi-faceted, non-linear modes of explanation, a different conception of society has to be found. This new conception will be comprised of many diverse elements and will constitute a change that can be seen to be as far-reaching as a paradigm shift (in Kuhnian terminology). A totally new structure of this type or a paradigm shift takes a long time to construct and much work needs to be done to explain, clarify and work out the blind alleys and unfruitful starting points for such a new approach. However, for the purposes of this summary, three elements of this new approach will be mentioned, elements that have direct bearing on the issues discussed in the preceding chapters. First, a reappraisal of how society is conceived; second, a critique of the mechanistic paradigm; and, third, a deconstruction of the epistemological position that divides subjects into different and discrete disciplines. This is not an exhaustive survey but enough for the present purpose to give an indication of ways forward and new beginnings.

The first necessary element in this reconception is a reappraisal of how society is conceptualized. The individualistic mechanisms that see society as an amalgam of separate, distinct individuals have never been conclusively refuted. These approaches conceived society as having a secondary ontological status, a status that gives it no existence independent of the individuals who make it up and hence ultimately no existence at all. On the other hand, the holists argued that society should be seen as an entity in its own right and have attempted to counter the reductionist view that society is incapable of explanation unless it has been reduced to its component parts and analyzed at that level. E Laszlo has argued that this reductionism is an inadequate conceptual tool that results in a bizarre view of society and one that has led it to be conceived in the following way:

> A set of objects related merely by spatial or mechanical adjacency is a heap, or conglomeration, of externally related, mutually independent units. It is a summative complex, for it is properly described by the summation of the individual parts. Taking away one part, or adding some, makes no difference to the character of the whole....Each part can be understood by itself; reference to the rest is not helpful or indicated. (1972:100)

This reductionist approach leads to an inadequate conceptual framework in which society cannot be analysed in terms of collective structures such as economic, political and legal frameworks, structures that cannot and should not be completely dismissed from the explanation process. In order to offer an alternative to this reductionist framework, holists have had to construct the concept of society in a manner that would make the idea of reductionism singly inappropriate. This was never achieved by traditional holism within social philosophy, because the problem of what ontological status to give society was never resolved - it always allowed reductionism in through the back door. Society was always kept as a purely theoretical structure and, due to the retention of the abstract individual as the central subject, its influence was never fully theorized.

One example of an alternative to the reductionist conception of society can be found in Laszlo's work, he provides an account of a move away from traditional ideas of society towards a more synthetic approach. Laszlo puts the analysis of society into a framework of systems, in which systems themselves are the object under study and these systems are given the status of coherent entities in their own right. Once this premise has been established, it is possible to interpret social behaviour in the context of a social system. This system will have some systemic irreducible properties of its own that cannot be determined by carving it up into single units and then examining them. For instance, a society will have characteristics, mores and cultures that will exist even if certain component parts leave or die. If there is a dramatic population fall it is likely that the character of a culture will change, but if, as in Western societies, only a small percentage die off each year, the essential character will remain constant. Thus, the mechanistic metaphor cannot be usefully applied to societies. The mechanistic principle, that if one part fails to cooperate the chain is broken and the whole system fails, is not applicable to natural systems, Laszlo states:

> Natural systems, however, are not like this. There are correlations between their input and outputs - between what you press and what pops up - but these are not deterministic ones. The components of natural systems form something like democracies in which it is agreed that certain functions will be carried out, but where it is left up to volunteers to fulfil them. It matters not in the least which particular component carries out a task. (1972b:113)

One important reason for this prevalent reductionism is an adherence to the principle of mechanism, which has served as a metaphor for social organizations. This mechanistic paradigm is the second element that needs reappraisal in the process of constructing a new paradigm. Mechanism grew out of and was made possible by the industrialization of the means of production. Its roots lay in the dualism of Descartes and as a concept it has progressed towards a more sophisticated analysis, beginning with the basic notion of clockwork and culminating in the formulation of disciplines such as electronics and computer technology.

Further, mechanism was applied to all facets of human existence; biology and hence medicine, society and natural sciences, were all formulated with a reliance on mechanistic metaphors. Organisms were reduced to their cellular and molecular mechanisms and it was argued that they were best studied by reference to their component parts. Hence, they were dissected and reduced to whatever sub-section interested the scientist. An exact specification of organisms took a long time to achieve as the authors of *Not In Our Genes* state:

> The mechanists could make programmatic statements about how life was reducible to chemistry, but these were largely acts of faith. Not until a century after the first non-organic synthesis of the simple body chemicals did the molecular nature and structures of the giant molecules begin to be resolved. (1985:47)

Despite the slow move towards actually achieving a concrete scientific basis for the explanation of organisms in a reductionist framework, the aim to account for all bodily processes in physiological terms continued unabated. Humanity also fell victim to this dissecting, reductionist approach; once the mechanistic metaphor was firmly established illness could be isolated in a single part of the body and treated accordingly.

As mentioned in Chapter Three, in order for mechanism and reductionism to flourish as a coherent body of thought, the origin of life had to be characterized within similar conceptual terms. This was achieved by Darwinian evolutionary theory. It introduced a key notion, that of time and with time, progress. All species could now be conceptualized as progressing from primitive stages towards more sophisticated and complex ways of life. In the same way that a machine is improved and calculators become smaller, faster, and cheaper, organisms also move towards efficiency. This notion of time firmly established the directional quality of life, in which causation became linear and was regarded as a natural phenomenon. There could be no looping back or regression as species flourished because their survival was based on pursuing the most productive and efficient evolutionary strategy.

This "survival of the fittest" reintroduced the concept of hierarchy into the system. Previously, the God-centred universe had legitimized inequalities, people were born into their roles and redemption and equality would be provided in heaven. With the Darwinian concept of natural selection a new type of hierarchy could be formulated. Species who were not maximizing their fitness would die out and be replaced by those who were more efficient and more able to adapt to prevailing conditions. This entrenched the idea that a notion of progress was inherent in biology itself. Such an idea of natural selection could also be applied to humans and it was held that traits and

130

characteristics not furthering the survival of the species would die out. Thus, the capitalistic mode of production, and the character forms it was built on, became, under this notion of natural selection, the optimum arrangement for the functioning of human societies. To be kind and helpful to others, to refuse to see profit as the final justification, would not maximize fitness and thus could be seen as evolutionary suicide.

Additionally, this concept of "survival of the fittest", functioned as a self-fulfilling prophecy. The form of human nature exhibited in modern, industrial society, could now be said to be the natural way humans are and consequently unchangeable. Further, it was also considered to be the optimum functioning of humanity, as this form of behaviour had evolved and was the highest point humanity had yet reached on the evolutionary scale. Communal living and sharing had withered away because they were inefficient mechanisms for the perpetuation of the species. In this way, the mechanistic paradigm flourished and the basis for biological determinist theories of human nature could be formalized.

If society is formulated to cohere with this mechanistic metaphor, the possibility of synthesis of any component parts is reduced. In order to overcome this mechanization of organic structures (from simple ones like bodies - to complex ones like societies) an analysis is needed that incorporates their dynamic and changing nature. As Capra states, "a fuller understanding of life will be achieved only by developing a "systems" biology', a biology that sees an organism as a living system rather than a machine." (1982:286) This will be comprised of an approach that integrates the various parts. In Capra's words again:

> All these natural systems are wholes whose specific structure arises from the interactions and inter-dependence of their parts. The activity of systems involves a process known as transaction - the simultaneous and mutually interdependent interaction between multiple components. Systemic properties are destroyed when a system is dissected, either physically or theoretically, into isolated elements. Although we can discern individual parts in any system, the nature of the whole is always different from the sum of its parts. (1982:287)

The mechanistic framework conceived entities as parts that operated in a precise and predetermined way - this can be replaced by notions of interdependence, flexibility and plasticity. Further, linear causation provides a good explanation of machines but it cannot be said to apply to organisms that operate in a cyclical pattern. For instance information processing can be understood as a cyclical procedure operating with information with feedback loops, a breakdown in one part will affect all the others by these loops and feedbacks and the original source of the trouble is often irrelevant. This has implications for biological determinism, evolutionary progression and methods of analysis,

131

and particularly in medicine, where such an approach would make the mechanistic search for disease in a single area redundant.

The final element that needs deconstruction for this new paradigm is the division of the world into different academic disciplines. The notion that spheres of knowledge can be divided up into separate parts clearly builds on these aforementioned mechanistic and reductionist principles. To study something adequately, all its inherent characteristics must be analysed, not simply those that relate to specific disciplinary concerns. Additionally, where the bisection is made is often a crucial decision, colouring the analysis from the outset. The most pertinent example of this segregation of knowledge is psychology, which has tried to emulate a positivist scientific structure to gain credence and has become unaware of the changing philosophical underpinnings of its position. The practical results of this segregation is the mechanistic and reductionist treatment regime that psychology employs. In addition, psychology is unable to meet the changing demands that are being made of it, such as a move away from psychology as a mechanism of control towards a mechanism of treatment and help.

This book has attempted to show that supposedly objective, abstract constructs have wide-ranging practical outcomes. They are part of a validation for the structures of society and political organization, rather than timeless, pre-existent entities. It has not tried to provide a conclusive way forward - just suggestions. That is the next stage.

# Notes

1.     For an elucidation of discourse theory, see: M,Foucault. (1972), *The Archaeology of Knowledge*, Tavistock Publications, London. Part II, "The Discursive Regularities". Also, by Foucault. (1970), *The Order of Things*, Tavistock Publications London. For an excellent commentary of these works, see: A,Sheridan. (1980), *The Will to Truth*, Tavistock Publications, London.

# Bibliography

Adorno, T.W. et al. (1950), *The Authoritarian Personality*, Harper, New York.

Alcroft, L. (1988), "Cultural Feminism Versus Poststructuralism", in *Signs*, 13, (31).

Allport, G.W. (1954), *The Nature of Prejudice*, Addison-Wesley, Massachusetts. The abridged version (1958), Anchor Books, New York.

Althusser, L. (1969), *For Marx*, (translated B.Brewster), Allen Lane, Penguin, London.
-(1976), *Essays in Self-Criticism*, (G Lode trans), New Left Books, London.

Armistead, N. (1974), (ed.), *Reconstructing Social Psychology*, Penguin, Harmondsworth.

Back, K.W. (1977), (ed.), *Social Psychology*, John Wiley & Sons Inc.

Ballard, R. (1979), "Ethnic Minorities & Social Services; what type of service?", in Khan.

Barash, D.P. (1977), *Sociobiology and Behaviour*, Elsevier, New York.

Barry, N. (1979), *Hayek's Social & Economic Philosophy*, Macmillian, London.

Bateson, G. (1979), *Mind & Nature*, Flamingo, London.

Bordo, S. (1990), "Feminism, Postmodernism and Gender - Sceptism", in Nicholson.

Braidotti, R. (1987), "Envy: or with my brains and your looks", in Jardine and Smith.

Bridenthal, R. & Koony, C. (1977), (ed.), *Becoming Visible*, Houghton Miffin, Boston.

Briody Mahowald, M. (1978), *Philosophy of Women: Classical to Current Concepts*, Hackett Publishing, Indianapolis.

Broadbent, D.E. (1973), *In Defense of Empirical Psychology*, Methuen, London.

*The Broadwater Farm Inquiry*, (1986), Kiria Press, London.

Brown, P.L. (1975), "Epistemology and Method: Althusser, Foucault, Derrida", *Cultural Hermenutics*, Vol 3, No 2.

Butler, J. (1990), *Gender Trouble*, Routledge, London.

Bynum, R. Porter, R. and Shepard, M. (1988), (ed.), *The Anatomy of Madness: Vol Three*, Routledge, London.

Canguilhem. (1975), "Physics of the External Senses", *Etudes d histoire et de Philosophie des Sciences*, Paris, Vrin.

Capra, F. (1982), *The Turning Point*, Flamingo, London.
-(1985), *The Tao of Physics*, Flamingo, London.

Castel, F. (1976), *L Ordre Psychiatrique*, Paris Editions de Minuit.

Chalmers, A. (1983), *What is this thing called Science?*, Open University Press, Milton Keynes.

Chodorow, N. (1978), *The Reproduction of Mothering*, Berkeley Univ. of Calif. Press, California.

Cochrane, R. (1977), "Mental illness in immigrants to England & Wales", *Social Psychiatry*, 12.

Cooley, C.H. (1912), *Human Nature and the Social Order*, New York.

Coulter, J. (1979), *The Social Construction of Mind*, Macmillian, London.

Diamond, I. & Quinby, L. (1988), (ed.), *Feminism & Foucault: Reflection on Resistance*, Northeastern University Press, Boston.

Dinnerstein, D. (1976), *The Mermaid & Minotaur*, Harper & Row, New York.

Di Stefano, C. (1990), "Dilemmas of Difference", in Nicholson.

Dorner, K. (1981), *Madmen & the Bourgeoisie*, Basil Blackwell, Oxford.

Dreyfus, H. & Rabinow, P. (1982), *Michel Foucault: Beyond Structuralism and Hermeneutics*, Harvester Wheatsheaf, London.

Durmout, L. (1965), "The Modern Conception of the Individual", *Contributions to Indian Sociology*, No V111, October.
-(1970), *Homo Hierarchicus*, Paladin, London.

Easlea, B. (1980), *Witchhunting, Magic and the New Philosophy*, Harvester, Brighton.

Elliott, G. (1988), *Althusser: The Detour of Theory*, Verso, London.

Elshtain, J.B. (1981), *Public Man, Private Women*, Martin Robertson, Oxford.

Eysenck, H.J. (1973), *The Uses & Abuses of Psychology*, Pelican, Harmondsworth.

Feinberg, J. (1973), *Social Philosophy*, Prentice-Hall, New Jersey.

Flax, J. (1983), "Political Philosophy and the Patriarchal Unconscious: A psychoanalytic perspective on epistemology and metaphysics", in Harding & Hintikka.

Foucault, M. (1965), *Madness & Civilization*, Tavistock Publications, London.
-(1970), *The Order of Things*, Tavistock Publications, London.
-(1971), "The Order of Discourse", in *Social Science Information*, Vol 10, No. 2.
-(1972), *The Archaeology of Knowledge*, Tavistock Publications, London.
-(1973), *The Birth of the Clinic*, Tavistock Publications, London.
-(1980), *Power/Knowledge: selected interviews & other writings*, 1972-77, Gordon, C. (ed.), Pantheon Books, New York.
-(1982), "Afterword", in Dreyfus and Rabinow.
-(1990), *The History of Sexuality, Vol 1: An Introduction*, Translated Robert Hurley, Penguin, Harmondsworth.
-(1991), *Discipline and Punish*, Penguin, Harmondsworth.

Frith, L.J. (1992), "Sociobiology, Ethics and Human Nature", in Lamb.

Fuss, D. (1990), *Essentially Speaking*, Routledge, London.

Gardiner, P. (1959), (ed.), *Theories of History*, Free Press, London.

Ginsberg, M. (1956), "The Individual and Society", in *On the Diversity of Morals*, London.

Gray, J. (1986), *Hayek on Liberty*, Basil Blackwell, Oxford.

Grimshaw, J. (1986), *Feminist Philosophers: Women's Perspectives on Philosophical Traditions*, Wheatsheaf Books, Brighton.

Grosz, E. (1990), "Contemporary Theories of Power and Subjectivity", in Gunew.

Gunew, S. (1990), *Feminist Knowledge*, Routledge, London.

Harding, S. & Hintikka, M. (1983), (ed.), *Discovering Reality*, D.Reidel Publishing Company, London.

Harre, R. & Secord, P.F. (1972), *The Explanation of Social Behaviour*, Blackwell, Oxford.

Harre, R. Clarke, D. DeCarlo, N. (1985), *Motives and Mechanisms*, Methuen, London.

Harris, I. (1992), "Individualism in its Indian Context". Unpublished paper.

Harrison, G. et al. (1985), "A prospective study of Severe Mental Disorder in Afro-Caribbean patients", in *Psychological Medicine* 18, (3).

Hartsock, N. (1990), "Foucault on Power: A Theory for Women?", in Nicholson.

Hayek, F.A. (1949), *Individualism & the Economic Order*, London.
-(1952), *The Counter Revolution of Science*, Glencoe, Ill.
-(1973), "Scientism and the Study of Society", in O'Neill.
-(1986), *The Road To Serfdom*, Ark Paperbacks, London.
-(1987), *The Sensory Order: An inquiry into the foundations of theoretical psychology*, Routledge & Kegan Paul, London.

Heath, S. (1978), "Differences", *Screen*, 19:3.

Heckman, S. (1990), *Gender and Knowledge*, Polity Press, Oxford.

Henriques, J. et al. (1984), *Changing the Subject*, Methuen, London & New York.

Hill, C. (1972*), The World Turned Upside Down: Radical ideas during the English Revolution*, Pelican, Harmondsworth.
-(1975), *Reformation to Industrial Revolution*, Pelican, Harmondsworth.

Hirst, P. & Woolley, P. (1982), *Social Relations & Human Attributes*, Tavistock Publications, London.

Hobsbawm, E.J. (1969), *Industry & Empire*, Pelican, Harmondsworth.

Hollis, M. & Lukes, S. (ed.), *Rationality and Relativism*, Basil Blackwell, Oxford.

Hooker, M. (1978), (ed.), *Descartes*, John Hopkins University Press, Baltimore.

Hull, C.L. (1943), *Principals of Behaviour*, Appleton-Century-Crofts, New York.

Ingleby, D. (1970), "Ideology and the human sciences", *Human Context*, 2.
-(1981), (ed.), *Critical Psychiatry: The Politics of mental health*, Penguin, Harmondsworth.

Jagger, A. (1983), *Feminist Politics and Human Nature*, Harvester, Brighton.

James, S. (1984), *The Content of Social Explanation*, Cambridge University Press, Cambridge.

Jardine, A. and Smith, P. (1987), (ed.), *Men in Feminism*, Methuen, London.

Jardine, A. (1987), "Men in Feminism", in Jardine and Smith.

Khan, V.S. (1979), *Minority Families in Britain*, MacMillan, London.

Khineberg, E. (1960), *Social Psychology*, Henry Holt & Co, New York.
-(1977), in Back.

Koch, S. (1964), "Psychology and Emerging Conceptions of Knowledge as Unitary", in Wann.

Krishnamurti. (1986), *The Impossible Question*, Penguin Books, Harmondsworth.
-(1987), *The Penguin Krishnamurti Reader*, Lutyens,M. (ed.), Penguin Books, Harmondsworth.

Kuhn, T.S. (1970), *The Structure of Scientific Revolutions*, University of Chicago Press,.

Lakatos, I. & Musgrave, A. (1970), (ed.), *Criticisms and the Growth of Knowledge*, Cambridge University Press.

Lamb, D. (1979), *Language and Perception in Hegel and Wittingstein*, Avebury, Amersham.
-(1992), (ed.), *New Horizons in the Philosophy of Science*, Avebury, Aldershot.

Larrain, J. (1979), *The Concept of Ideology*, Hutchinson and Co Ltd, London.

Laszlo, E. (1972), *The Systems View of the World*, George Braziller, New York.
-(1972b), *Introduction to Systems Philosophy*, Gordon & Breach Science Publishers, London.
-(1987), *Evolution: The grand synthesis*, New Science Library.

Lichtheim, G. (1967), *The Concept of Ideology and other Essays*, Random House.

Lindsey, G. & Aronson, G. (1986), (ed.), *The Handbook of Social Psychology Vol V*, Addison-Wesley, Massachusetts.

Littlewood, R. (1981), "Some Social & Phenomenological characteristics of psychotic immigrants", *Psychological Medicine*, 11.

Littlewood, R. & Lipsedge, M. (1982), *Aliens & Alienists: Ethnic Minorities in Psychiatry*, Penguin, Harmondsworth.

Lloyd, G. (1984), *The Man of Reason: Male & Female in Western Philosophy*, Methuen, London.

Lukes, S. (1985), *Individualism*, Basil Blackwell, Oxford.

Mackie, J.L. (1982), *the Miracle of Theism*, Oxford University Press.

Macpherson, C.B. (1964), *The Political Theory of Possessive Individualism*, Oxford University Press, Oxford.

Major, J. (1991), Speech to Conservative Party Conference in Blackpool.

Major-Poetzl, P. (1983), *Michel Foucault's Archaeology of Western Culture*, The Harvester Press, Brighton.

Mandelbaum. (1973), "Societal Facts", in O'Neill.

Marbable, M. (1985), *Black American Politics*, Verso, London.

Marquand, D. (1990), "Collective Spirit Versus Individual Ambitions", in *The Guardian*, 15th October.

McGovan, D. & Cope, R.V. (1987), "First Psychiatric admissions rates of first & second generation Afro-Caribbeans", *Social Psychiatry*, 22.

McNay, L. (1992), *Foucault and Feminism*, Polity, Oxford.

Margolis, J. (1984), *Philosophy of Psychology*, Prentice Hall, Englewood Cliffs, N.J.

Mercer, K. (1986), "Racism & transcultural psychiatry", in Miller and Rose.

Merchant, C. & Dijksterhuis, E.J. (ed.), (1961), *The Mechanization of the World Picture*, Clarendon Press.
-(1979), *The Death of Nature: women, ecology, and the scientific revolution*, Harper & Row, London.

Meszaros, I. (1986), *Philosophy Ideology & Social Science: Essays in negation & affirmation*, Wheatsheaf Books, Sussex.

Miller, P. & Rose, N. (1986), (ed.), *The Power of Psychiatry*, Polity Press, London.

Miller, R. (1978), "Methodological Individualism", *Philosophy of Science*, 45.

Mishler, E.G. et al. (1981), (ed.), *Social Contexts of Health, Illness, & Patient Care*, Cambridge University Press, Cambridge.

Mitchell, J. (1975), *Psychoanalysis & Feminism*, Vintage Books, New York.

Myers, D. (1993), *Social Psychology*, McGraw-Hill Inc, New York.

Nicholson, L. (1990), (ed.), *Feminism/Postmodernism*, Routledge, London.

Ollman, B. (1971), *Alienation: Marx's conception of man in capitalist society*, Cambridge University Press, Cambridge.

O'Neill, J. (1973), (ed.), *Modes of Individualism & Collectivism*, Heinmann, London.

Pasquino, P. (1980), "Criminology: the birth of a special saviour" *Ideology and Consciousness*, 7.

Peacock, A. (1985), (ed.), *Reductionism in Academic Disciplines*, Srheanfer-Nelson.

Pecheux, M. (1975), *Les Verites de la Police*, Mespero, Paris.

Plamenatz, J. (1971), *Ideology*, Macmillan, London.
-(1975), *Karl Marx's Philosophy of Man*, Oxford University Press, Oxford.

Popper, K.R. (1965), "Social Science & Social Policy", in Braybrooke,D. (ed.), *Philosophical Problems of the Social Sciences*, Macmillan, New York.
-(1969), *The Poverty of Historicism*, Routledge & Kegan Paul, London.
-(1977), *The Open Society & its Enemies*, Vol.1&2, Routledge & Kegan Paul, London.

Poster, M. (1984), *Foucault, Marxism & History*, Polity Press, Cambridge.

Quinton, A. (1975-6), "Social Objects", *Proceedings of the Aristotelian Society*, 75.

Rajchman, J. (1991), *Truth and Eros*, Routledge, London.

Ranger, C. (1989), "Race, Culture & Cannabis Psychosis: the role of social factors in the construction of a disease category", *New Community*, Vol 15, No.3.

Rawls, J. (1972), *A Theory of Justice*, Oxford University Press, Oxford.

Richards, M. (1974), (ed.), *The Integration of a Child in the Social World*, Cambridge University Press, Cambridge.

Rose, S. et al. (1985), *Not in Our Genes*, Penguin, London.

Rubin, G. (1975), "The Traffic in Women: Notes on the "Political Economy" of Sex", in Reiter,R. (ed.), *Toward an Anthropology of Women*, Monthly Review Press, New York.

Ryan, A. (1979), (ed.), *The Idea of Freedom: Essays in Honour of Isaiah Berlin*, Oxford University Press, Oxford
-(1984*), The Philosophy of the Social Sciences*, Macmillan, London.

*The Scarman Report: The Brixton Disorder* April 1981, Cmnd 8427.

Scheman, N. (1983), "Individualism and the Objects of Psychology", in Harding and Hintikka.

Scidentop, L. (1979), "Two Liberal Tradition", in Ryan.

Sedgwick, P. (1982), *Psycho Politics*, Harper & Row, New York.

Seve, L. (1978), *Man in Marxist Theory and the Psychology of Personality*, Harvester, Brighton.

Sheridan, A. (1980), *Michel Foucault: The Will to Truth*, Tavistock Publications, London.

Shotter, J. (1974), "What is it to be Human", in Armistead.
-(1974a), *Images of man in Psychological Research*, Methuen, London.
-(1974b), "The Development of Social Power", in Richards.

Singer, P. (1981), *The Expanding Circle*, Farrar, New York.

Smart, B. (1985), *Michel Foucault*, Ellis Horwood Ltd, Chichester.

Sommers, F. (1978), "Dualism in Descartes", in Hooker.

Soper, K. (1990), *Troubled Pleasures*, Verso, London.

Spender, D. (1980), *Man-Made Language*, Routledge & Kegan Paul, London.
-(1982*), Women of Ideas (and what men have done to them)*, Routledge & Kegan Paul, London.

Spivak, G. (1987), *In Other Worlds*, Methuen, London.

Szasz, T. (1979), *The Myth of Psychotherapy*, Oxford University Press, Oxford.

Tajfel, H. et al. (1971), "Social Categorization & Intergroup Behaviour", *European Journal of Social Psychology*, 1, (1).

Venn, C. (1984), "The Subject of Psychology", in Henriques.

Taylor, H.F. (1980), *The IQ Game*, Rutgers University Press, New Jersey.

142

Wann, T.W. (1964), (ed.), *Behaviourism and Phenomenology*, Chicago University Press.

Watkins, J.W.N. (1959), "Historical Explanation in the Social Sciences", in Gardiner, P. (ed.), *Theories of History*, Free Press, London.
-(1973), "Ideal Types and Historical Explanations", in O'Neill

Wilson, E.O. (1975), *Sociobiology: The New Synthesis*, Belnap, Cambridge Mass.

Wintour, P. (1991), "How Majorism took the "I" out of "isms"" in *The Guardian*, 25th March.

Wolff, R.P. (1968), *The Poverty of Liberalism*, Beacon Press.

Wunt, W.M. (1907), *Outline of Psychology*, W. Engleman, Leipzig.
-(1973), *The Language of Gestures*, The Hague, Morton.

Young, I. (1990), "The Ideal of Community and the Politics of Difference." in Nicholson.

Young, M. & Willmott, P. (1962), *Family and Kinship in East London*, Pelican, Harmondsworth.